For Those Who Never Danced

Ruth Carney

TRILOGY
A WHOLLY OWNED SUBSIDIARY OF TBN
PROFESSIONAL PUBLISHING MEETS POWERFUL PROMOTION

Trilogy Christian Publishers

A Wholly Owned Subsidiary of Trinity Broadcasting Network
2442 Michelle Drive
Tustin, CA 92780
Copyright © 2024 by Ruth Carney

All Scripture quotations, unless otherwise marked, are taken from THE HOLY BIBLE, NEW INTERNATIONAL VERSION®, NIV® Copyright © 1973, 1978, 1984, 2011 by Biblica, Inc.® Used by permission. All rights reserved worldwide.

Scripture quotations marked AMP are taken from the Amplified® Bible, Classic Addition (AMPC), Copyright © 2015 by The Lockman Foundation. Used by permission. www.Lockman.org.

Scripture quotations marked ASV are taken from the American Standard Version of the Bible, 1901. Public domain.

Scripture quotations marked BSB are taken from the The Holy Bible, Berean Standard Bible, BSB Copyright ©2016, 2020 by Bible Hub Used by Permission. All Rights Reserved Worldwide.

Scripture quotations marked ESV are taken from the ESV® Bible (The Holy Bible, English Standard Version®), copyright © 2001 by Crossway Bibles, a publishing ministry of Good News Publishers. Used by permission. All rights reserved.

Scripture quotations marked KJV, are taken from The Holy Bible, King James Version. Cambridge Edition: 1769.

All rights reserved, including the right to reproduce this book or

portions thereof in any form whatsoever.
For information, address Trilogy Christian Publishing
Rights Department, 2442 Michelle Drive, Tustin, CA 92780.
Trilogy Christian Publishing/ TBN and colophon are trademarks of
Trinity Broadcasting Network.
For information about special discounts for bulk purchases, please
contact Trilogy Christian Publishing.

Trilogy Disclaimer: The views and content expressed in this book are those of the author and may not necessarily reflect the views and doctrine of Trilogy Christian Publishing or the Trinity Broadcasting Network.

10 9 8 7 6 5 4 3 2 1
Library of Congress Cataloging-in-Publication Data is available.
ISBN 979-8-89333-100-4
ISBN 979-8-89333-101-1

Table of Contents

DEDICATION V
INTRODUCTION 1

CHAPTER 1
Haven't I Told You a Thousand Times? 5

CHAPTER 2
Woman, Why Are You Weeping? 11

CHAPTER 3
"They Took Away My Jesus...and I Don't Know Where They Put Him!" .16

CHAPTER 4
Chicken Farms and Other Institutes of Higher Learning 20

CHAPTER 5
Dark Mirror on the Wall, Who's the Sick One After All? 31

CHAPTER 6
Moats, Beams, and Other Optical Obstacles! 40

CHAPTER 7
This Earth Is Not My Home, Or Vapors and Other Aliens 43

CHAPTER 8
Final Destination and Taking Care of the Inheritance 53

CHAPTER 9
When You Don't Pay Attention, You Get Into Trouble! 61

CHAPTER 10
REST, STRESS, or OUT OF CONTROL! 66

CHAPTER 11
The Virtuous Woman—"Who, ME?" 72

CHAPTER 12
The Journey Home—My Story! Well, It's Really His-Story 80

CHAPTER 13
He Put a New Song in My Heart—A Song of Praise 90

CHAPTER 14
A Good Name 94

THE FINAL CHAPTER OR ADDENDUM 108
About the Author 116
Endnotes 117

DEDICATION

This book is dedicated to the most wonderful family any person could have. First, in memory of my mother, Tommie Lee Glenn Wheat, and my father, Samuel Houston Wheat. My awesome husband Kenneth Ray Carney has been my rock, my teacher, my "trainer," my partner through it all. There would have been no story to tell without him. Have you ever thought about the fact that if you had not married the person you married, all your children and grandchildren would not exist? Horrible thought! So to my sons, their wives, and their children, I not only dedicate this book but the rest of my life and all my earthly goods! I'm not cleaning out closets—I'm leaving it all to you!

Michael married Jewl and had one boy, Shine, and one girl, Free. They both have Hawaiian middle names, which I cannot spell nor pronounce! Barry married Charlotte and had Alyssa, who married Declan Weir and lives in Scotland. Alex, who needs a wife. Andrew, who married Katie and had Sophie, Aodhan, and Benjamin. Christopher, our third born, married Tiffany and had Kenneth James (KJ) and Bentley. Greg, our fourth son, married Sarah and had Phoenix and Shiloh. So far, we have nine grandchildren and three great grandchildren. Maybe more to come? I am abundantly blessed beyond anything I could ask or imagine!

As the breeze gently persuades its countless seeds to embark on a journey of renewal and growth, each seed floats gracefully, carrying the plant's legacy into the unknown. This tranquil moment beautifully encapsulates nature's elegant and continuous dance between life and rebirth.

INTRODUCTION

"Thou hast turned for me my mourning into dancing" (Psalm 30:11).

"To everything there is a season, and a time to every purpose under the heaven: A time to weep, and a time to laugh, a time to mourn, and a time to dance" (Ecclesiastes 3:1, 4).

For some reason, the title came to me before the book was written. I always said, "If I ever write a book, the title will be *"For Those Who Never Danced."* That's me. I never danced—at least not where anyone saw me. I don't know how many people this will relate to. Maybe I'm the only one. What a depressing thought! Maybe the reason I never danced, or one of the reasons, was that I was told that I couldn't. I was told I couldn't cut my hair, wear jewelry, put on makeup, go swimming (well, it was called "mixed bathing" back then), or wear shorts or slacks. I don't understand why the dancing part stuck while the others slowly but surely were partaken of without as much as one little earthquake or a thunderbolt and lightening flash. It could be because I missed those early formative years of development, you know, the eye hand coordination, or maybe it was the foot-brain part I missed. Whatever it was, I was told I couldn't and I believed I couldn't. It had a paralyzing effect on me.

Oh, I've never had a desire to dance those vulgar, seductive dances to the loud beat of a hard rock band. I've only desired to flow, move with the rhythm and melody of violins and saxophones, or perhaps as a child leaps in a

1

For Those Who Never Danced

dance of delight as the waves splash against the shoreline, or to dance with the wind on a mountain peak to the sound of music.

Many of us have been paralyzed by what we have been told and accepted as truth. For that reason, I've told my kids, "Yes! You can dance!" I enjoy watching them dance the meringue or salsa which they learned while we lived in the Dominican Republic, a place where people literally dance in the streets.

I don't ever want to be the one who paralyzes another human being. Oh, how careful we must be with our rules and regulations. Dancing is like fire or water or sex or anything else in this world. It was designed by God. It can free us or destroy us. Fire can warm us or burn us. Water can quench our thirst or drown us. Sex can be the expression of love and the means by which we were all created and given life, or it can represent rape, abuse, or abortions.

Until I started trying to make sense of the title of this book, or justify it, I didn't realize how closely related *dancing* and *grace* are. Here are some definitions:

- Dance:
- To *move* the body and feet in *rhythm,* ordinarily to music
- To be stirred into rapid movement as *"leaves in a wind"*
- To *move* lightly and gaily
- Dance to another tune, i.e. to alter one's actions or opinions as a result of changed conditions
- Grace:
- Beauty or charm of form, composition, *movement*, or expression
- The unmerited love and favor of God toward man

(That's enough to make you dance!)
- Movement:
- Same as tempo or rhythm or motion
- Rhythmic flow
- To change the place or position of

My favorite definition of dance is *"to be stirred into rapid movement as leaves in a wind."*

> As for man, his days are as grass,
> As the flower of the field, so he flourisheth.
> for the wind passeth over it and it is gone.
> and the place thereof shall know it no more.
> Psalm 103:15–16

> But we are all as an unclean thing and all our righteousness are as filthy rags and we all do fade as a leaf, and our iniquities like the wind, have taken us away.
> Isaiah 64:6

> We spend our years as a tale that is told,
> so teach us to number our days
> that we may apply our hearts unto wisdom
> and let the beauty of the Lord our God be upon us
> and establish thou the work of our hands upon us,
> Yes!
> The work of our hands establish thou it!
>
> Psalm 90:9, 12, 17

This book is really *a tale that must be told.* It's about grass and flowers and leaves and wind and liquids and solids. It's about people and places and movement and change and lessons learned. It's about grace and beauty and weeping and laughter and dancing to the rhythm of a million different melodies that life has orchestrated. But mostly it's about the Word that was made flesh and dwelt among us, full of GRACE and TRUTH.

And now it's *"time to dance."*

CHAPTER 1

Haven't I Told You a Thousand Times?

"When will you do what you've been told?"
"I've told you time and time again,
but you never listen!"
"Don't you hear me?"
"Can't you see what needs to be done?"
"Could you just walk over this garbage all day and
never pick it up?"
"What's it going to take? A time bomb?
An earthquake?"
"You aren't listening to me!"
"Pay attention and you'll learn."
"If you do what you're told,
you won't get   hurt!"
"What is it about 'NO' that you don't
understand?"
"Son, you're twelve years old now. This means for the
last ten years I've been telling you to
LIFT THE LID!"

Do these words sound familiar to you? If you're a parent, you use them quite often. If you're a kid, you probably hear them more than you would like to, not that you pay any attention! It's probably just a low mumbling that occurs mostly in the early evening up until about bedtime.

Would you like to know why we have children? Maybe some of you already know, others are still trying to figure it out. No, it has nothing to do with birds and bees, and has everything to do with God's revenge. You see, it's the only way we will ever learn some of life's most important lessons. There's absolutely no other way to learn them so those of you who have no children can borrow mine. It is, to be quite exact, God's way of letting us know the extreme frustration *He* feels with *us adults*. He says it pretty much the same way we do. Now listen to this:

> Though seeing, they do not see;
> Though hearing, they do not hear or understand,
> In them is fulfilled the prophecy of Isaiah:
> You will be ever hearing but never understanding.
> You will be ever seeing but never perceiving.
> For this people's heart has become callused.
> They hardly hear with their ears
> and they have closed their eyes.
> Otherwise they might see with their eyes,
> hear with their ears,
> understand with their hearts
> and turn, and I would heal them.
>
> Mathew 13:13–15

Another version says it this way:

"Having eyes you see NOT. Having ears you hear NOT" (Mark 8:18).

The problem is, we've been seeing in the NOTS! The negatives. And mostly, we see "HIM" NOT.

We see Him NOT as the Everlasting God, the Lord, the Creator of the ends of the earth. We see Him NOT as the God in charge of our lives, who cares for us better than we can care for ourselves. So we find ourselves acting like our own children, having to be told time and time again and

Chapter 1

having to relearn the lessons we thought we had already learned and then learn them again. That's why God gave me Greg. He's the youngest of our four boys and the philosopher of the family. He's the one who will look me right in the eyes and say, "It's just not fair Mom, you know it's wrong. You know it shouldn't be done this way." And he is usually right!

It was one of those usual hot, muggy afternoons in the Dominican Republic, with the breeze blowing through our back door and out the front door as the ceiling fans were trying to circulate the air. I entered the living room and found eight-year-old Greg visibly (and audibly) upset. He hates for me to say he was crying but his face was wet. I looked at him with concern and said, "Greg, what is wrong? What happened?"

Expecting to hear a war story between him and his brother Chris, I was surprised when he said, "It's Dad. He won't let me give away my shoes!" And the tears fell on his face again.

With all my logic and reason, I said, "But Greg, you only have two pairs of shoes, one for school and one pair to play in the jungle! If you give your jungle pair away, you cannot wear your school shoes to play in and you know we don't go back to the States for several months to buy clothes. These shoes have to last." I was firm and felt I had explained it to him in a way which he could understand.

His eyes pierced through me and he firmly and logically said, "It's just not fair. I have two pairs of shoes and Tito, my friend, has none. He has never had a pair of tennis shoes and YOU told me to 'do unto others as you would have them do unto you,' and if you had never had a pair of shoes, you would want somebody to give you theirs!"

How could I argue? I had been told that a thousand times. I had even taught my children to "do unto others

7

as you would have them do unto you." So why had I not learned it yet? Why do I have to be such a slow learner! I looked at him with compassion and embarrassment and said, "Go, Greg…go give them away!"

And he did, and in so doing, he opened a channel of blessing that was unbelievable! He and his brother Chris would "sneak" out the front door with clothes behind their backs, and I would later see kids playing in the streets with their shirts on. One day, I caught Chris with a brand-new shirt and said, "Chris, that's your new shirt. You can't give that away." And he looked at me with the same disbelief that God does and said, "They never get new shirts Mom, they always get the old used ones!" I heard God speak so loudly that I hope I never have to be told again:

"Give, [Ruth] and it shall be given unto you. Good measure, pressed down, shaken together and running over shall men give unto you. For with the same measure that you give, It will be measured to you again" (Luke 6:38). "Anyone who has two shirts should share with the one who has none, and anyone who has food should do the same" (John 3:11, NIV). It was the neighbors who shared their food with us, arroz con pollo (the chicken cooked with its head, eyeballs, beak, and feet with toenails)! It became our boys' favorite meal.

Most of you are fortunate enough to have a mailbox attached to your house, or at least beside your driveway. In the Dominican Republic, we had to drive downtown to the YWAM (Youth With A Mission) office to pick up the mail that was flown in on the private plane once a week, hopefully, if there weren't mechanical problems. We always looked forward to boxes. That meant someone had sent us some really nice things. You probably wouldn't get excited about things like baking soda (I waited three months for the local stores to get it in), or spray starch, or Pledge, face cream, lotion, dish liquid that was soapy, soft toilet tissue, and pretty napkins with designs on them. Sometimes it was chocolate chips, a box of cereal, or a few magazines in English. These things we learned to really appreciate and for which we were very grateful. But shortly after the shoe lesson from Greg and the shirt lesson from Chris, we received a BIG box. Anyone want to guess what was inside?

You're right! *Shoes and shirts!* The channel was flowing! Soon we had a deal with Leo, a friend in Puerto Rico who had connections with Foot Locker. He just happened to get a whole truckload of outdated, damaged, mis-sown, or mis-glued Nikes, Air Jordans, Reeboks, and every other brand-name shoe, and we got enough for everybody in our whole village. Even the ninety-eight-year-old grandma (I'm not sure how old she was exactly, but she looked ninety-eight) who lived across the street had the first pair of tennis shoes in her whole life!

Now, the baseball team that played in the cow pasture wearing flip-flops or, more amazingly, barefooted, were all fitted with shoes. That's why the Dominican professional players are so good. They learned to play baseball in a cow pasture, barefooted, with a homemade bat and no gloves. When the recruits come by and give them a ballfield, shoes, and a real bat, we watch them on TV. Juan Guzman, Pedro, and Ramon Martinez are from our little neighborhood in San Miguel. That reminds me of the baseball cap story.

I saw a kid walking down the road with the ball cap Chris just "had to have" for Christmas. The kind that is fitted—it doesn't snap—it costs more. I said (as usual), "Chris, that guy has on your new cap!" Chris said, "I know, I gave it to him; it doesn't fit me anymore." I knew that wasn't right because that guy was twenty and Chris was only twelve. Then he said, "Mom, he plays on a team and he's never had a hat."

Would you like to guess what started coming in the boxes?

My children had to teach me the lessons I should have already known. We are to be channels of God's blessings. He never gives to us selfishly. He gives, so that we can give, so that He can give. Many of us have stockpiles of clothes and shoes and things that somebody needs and we keep them in our closets and garages and rented storage buildings just in case we lose weight or the Stock market fails and all the department stores go out of business and because "we may need that someday."

And we pass people in our hurry/rush of every day and never realize that they have need of what we have…and we have need of what He has…and we stay such needy people…because we don't do what we've been told!

By the way, wouldn't you like to hear about the major surgeries I had while we lived overseas? Over the first ten years, I underwent three major, critical surgeries: eye surgery, ear surgery, and heart surgery. Having eyes, I didn't see, having ears, I didn't hear, and I understood with my head instead of my heart. I was a critically ill person. My journey to healing is what I'd like to share with you. Or, on the other hand, maybe I just want to help you learn how to dance! Remember the definition of dance? "Dance to another tune, to alter one's actions or opinions as a result of changed conditions."

CHAPTER 2

Woman, Why Are You Weeping?

If we could just stop *seeing NOT! Or stop not seeing!* It seems to be increasingly harder for us to see beyond our own needs to hear the desperation in the voices around us and around the world, to understand our own purpose for living, and to know that our own healing lies within our ability to *SEE, HEAR, and UNDERSTAND.*

John 20:11–13 (ASV) tells the story of Mary Magdalene. It's amazing how many of us can identify with Mary: "Mary was standing outside the tomb weeping, And so, as she wept, she stopped and looked into the tomb. And she beheld two angels and they said to her, 'Woman, why are you weeping?'"

I HATE IT WHEN MY HUSBAND CALLS ME "WOMAN." Especially when he says, *"WOMAN, WHY ARE YOU WEEPING?"* And he says it a lot because I weep—a lot! I love that scripture that talks about God keeping all our tears in a bottle. Well, He had to transfer mine to a cistern!

I hope you can keep up with me now. I'm going to start jumping around a bit, but we will come back to Mary.

> The Lord has done great things for us, whereof we are glad.
> Turn again [reverse] our captivity [things that keep us in bondage], O Lord
> As the streams in the South [that happens to be Tennessee right now!]

For Those Who Never Danced

> They that sow in tears shall reap in joy.
> He [she] that, goes fourth weeping, bearing precious seed shall doubtless come again with rejoicing, bringing [her] sheaves [bundles of grain, harvest] with [her].
>
> Psalms 126:3–5

[you'll notice that most of the scripture quotations will be From the "New Southern Version according to Ruth"]

> You number my wanderings:
> Put my tears into your bottle:
> Are they not in your book?
>
> Psalms 56:8

The rain was pouring as I sat beside the large windows in our great room, which overlooks the forest in which we live. (I'm referring to our squirrel farm in Tennessee; we can't afford cattle, and I bet you're wondering how I got from the Dominican Republic to Tennessee—I've been wondering, too!) The rain was gently but steadily falling on the leaves and making its impact in the small puddles that gently flowed together into a stream…

which lead to the big puddle at the bottom of the hill,

    which flows into a larger stream to the creek…

    which flows into a larger stream.

For some reason that day the raindrops looked *strangely* familiar, especially the ones pouring off the top of the car, down the windshield,

    over the hood and

        onto the ground, into the puddle

>which flows to the stream,
>
>>that has the hole in the bottom
>
>>>and the log and the frog!

They looked so familiar (the raindrops, not the frogs) that they actually brought tears to my eyes

>which flowed over my cheeks
>
>>down my chin
>
>>>and into my lap.

Could it be? Is it possible? Were those my tears? I've often wondered what He did with all those bottles of tears up there. He's never wasteful. He always puts things to good use. I know he has gallons of just mine! My mom used to say I had a tender heart.

It was back in the early '50s when I was a very small child. We were at my grandma's house. She had a TV and we didn't. It was the first time I had ever seen "big time wrestling," and I cried! How could people be so mean?

It had gotten so bad (crying) by the time I was seven. I remember praying that God would stop all the tears because I sure couldn't. I prayed this while I was sitting in a funeral service for my Uncle Spence, who lived in Atlanta. He had lung cancer and was in so much pain that he committed suicide. When we got there, the night after he died, we had to sleep in the room where he did it. As I sat in the chapel that day, I truly could not stop the tears from falling, but when I prayed for God to stop them, fear came over me. What if He did, and what if my heart wouldn't be tender or let me be sad anymore?

There were lots of funerals after that. (I had lots of uncles.) I experienced many more deaths of people. My grandma, my mom, my dad, my brother, my child, and deaths of dreams and hopes. I've watched a lot of movies since then and the tears have never stopped. I've even been known to cry while watching cartoons. Did you see *The Fox And The Hound*? My boys would always check to see if Mom was crying, and if she was, that was the okay for a good-ole-family-cry-out. Pass the tissues please.

I guess if God Himself won't stop my tears, there must be a purpose for them. Maybe He does recycle them...

To fall gently to the ground

  to nourish and bring forth new life

    (or at least a new way of living)

      and purpose (a new reason for living)

        and to help things grow (mostly me)

          and bloom (into the person he intended me to be)

            and to sustain life (tears are an emotional release,

              kind of like a sprinkler system) used when

                the heat and drought come, then our small

              puddles can make bigger puddles

            that make rivers of living water,

              that nourish other people who cry.

      Kind of like "weeping with those who weep"

                        (Romans 12:15).

For as the heavens are higher than the earth
So are my ways higher than your ways.
And my thoughts than your thoughts.
For as the rain [recycled tears] come down

And the snow from heaven
And do not return there but water the earth
And make it bring forth and bud
That it may give seed to the sower and bread to the eater
So shall my word be that goes forth from my mouth,
It shall not return unto me void
But it shall accomplish that which I please and it shall prosper
In the thing for which I sent it.
For you shall go out with joy
And be led forth with peace.
The mountains and hills shall break forth before you
into singing and all the trees of the field shall clap their hands!

Isaiah 55:8–12

"You have turned for me my mourning into dancing" (Psalm 30:11).

CHAPTER 3

"They Took Away My Jesus…

and I Don't Know Where They Put Him!"

> When she had said this, she turned around, and beheld Jesus standing there, and did not know that it was Jesus.
> Jesus said to her, "Woman, why are you weeping? Whom are you seeking?"
> Assuming Him to be the gardener, she said to Him, "Sir if you have carried him away, take me where you have laid Him, and I will take Him away."
> Jesus said to her, "Mary!"
> She turned and said to him, "Master!"
>
> John 20:14–16

We sit by the tomb too, you know. The tomb where we have buried our dreams, hopes, desires, and our crumbled lives.

Why do we weep? For the same reason Mary did. Someone, maybe we know them, maybe we don't, but it was someone. THEY, we blame them; it was their fault. They took away our Jesus, and we don't know where they put Him! *We lost our Lord! Someone has taken Him away!* We do the same thing that Adam did in the garden. We blame someone else. It's their fault that I'm crying!

Chapter 3

I read it somewhere many years ago. I wrote it down and put it on my refrigerator so I could see it every day. Then I memorized it and twenty-nine refrigerators later, it's a vital part of my life. Here it is—you should do the same.

"It's not life and its circumstances that need to change— ONLY THE SELF IN ME!"

We face each day either in the spirit of the tomb or the spirit of the Resurrection. Mary was just what the scripture described. "Having eyes you see not." She looked right at Jesus and didn't recognize Him.

"That I may know Him and the power of His Resurrection!" (Philippians 3:10).

That same resurrection power is available to us when He lives in us and His spirit guides us.

You've seen Him also and didn't recognize Him. You might have thought that was "just the gardener." Or just the grocery checkout boy or the service station attendant, or the neighbor next door. or maybe you thought He was just the beggar on the street.

> "Lord, when did we see you hungry and not feed you, or thirsty and not give you something to drink? When did we see you a stranger and not invite you in or needing clothes and not clothe you. When did we see you sick or in prison and not visit you?"
>
> Then shall He answer them saying, "In as much as you did it NOT to one of the least of these, you did it NOT to me!"
>
> Matthew 25:44–45

Sounds like we're still seeing Him *NOT*... in the faces of

those around us. We sing a lot of songs about waiting to see Jesus…someday.

"When we All Get to Heaven,

What a day of rejoicing that will be.

When we all see Jesus, we'll sing and shout the victory."

If we would just open our eyes, we would see Jesus all around us every day! There would be more singing and shouting the victory today, right now on this earth! We sing about Jesus *"High and Lifted Up,"*

> but if we don't learn to see Him….
>
> > crippled,
> >
> > > and blind,
> > >
> > > > and broken…
> > > >
> > > > > we probably won't recognize Him when we get to
> > > > >
> > > > > > heaven!

Mary may not have recognized Jesus when she saw Him, but she was at least listening when He spoke her name. And if we will always listen for His voice, we will hear Him speak our name, too. Mary, Ruth, Sarah, Matthew, Paul, and when He speaks our name, we will know for sure that *no one* can take away our Jesus. He is always there beside us and desires to be *in* us and for us to be *in Him*.

"Though he is not far from any one of us. For in him we live and move and have our being" (Acts 17:27–28).

"And you are complete in Him" (Colossians 2:10).

"I will never leave you or forsake you" (Hebrews 13:5).

Chapter 3

"Hear O Lord when I cry with my voice! Have mercy also upon me, and answer me. When you said, 'seek my face,' my heart said to you, 'Your face Lord, I will seek" (Psalm 27:7–8, KJV).

CHAPTER 4

Chicken Farms and Other Institutes of Higher Learning

I should have told you earlier, but it's something that I don't talk about a lot. You see, I'm a *chicken farmer's daughter from Georgia!* Sounds like a good title for a movie or a book or something, huh? Well, those kinds of people never get out. They stay there forever. Same house, same car, (10,000 miles in a lifetime), same rocking chair, same everything. I'm still wondering how I got out! I know what you're thinking. "What's this got to do with recognizing Jesus when you see him?" You'd be surprised!

I had a wonderful mom. She started teaching me the Word when I was a small child. Things like:

"Trust in the Lord with all your heart and lean not on your own understanding, In all your ways acknowledge Him and He will direct your path" (Proverbs 3:5–6).

Then there was:

> Delight yourself also in the Lord,
> And He will give you the desires and secret petitions of your heart.
> *Commit* your way to the Lord;
> *Trust* also in Him, and *He* will bring it to pass.
> *Be still* and *rest* in the Lord;
> *Wait patiently* for Him and
> *Fret not yourself*

Chapter 4

> But those who *wait* upon the Lord shall *inherit the earth.*
>
> Psalm 37:4–9

So I did just that. I took it literally. I kept it simple. I did what I was told. I trusted. I acknowledged Him. I delighted, committed, rested, and waited, and I fretted not. Now I just sit around and wonder what *in the world* to do with this inheritance! (More about that later.)

Let me tell you about those *desires and secret petitions* first.

Remember *Gilligan's Island*? I think they have reruns somewhere. I used to watch it and dream about living on a beautiful island in the Caribbean with those awesome palm trees, the beach, the sun, the sand. But… I was a chicken farmer's daughter in Georgia, and I knew those were places I'd probably never see. And the thought of being on anything faster than a tractor or a pickup truck, like an airplane or even a boat—far out!

> You have searched me, Lord, and you know me.
> You know when I sit and when I rise;
> You perceive my thoughts from afar (far out)
> You discern my going out and my lying down;
> You are familiar with all my ways.
> Before a word is on my tongue you Lord, know it completely (Oh Lord!)
> You hem me in behind and before, and lay your hand upon me.
> Such knowledge is too wonderful for me, too lofty for me to attain.
> Where can I flee from your presence? If I go up to the heavens, you are there;
> If I make my bed in the depths, you are there.

> If I rise on the wing of the dawn, if I settle on the far side of the sea,
> even there your hand will guide me, your right hand will hold me fast!
> If I say, "Surely the darkness will hide me and the light become night around me,"
> even the darkness will not be dark to you; the light will shine like the day,
> for darkness is as light to you.
> For you created my inmost being; you knit me together in my mother's womb.
> I praise you because I am fearfully and wonderfully made;
> your works are wonderful, I know that full well.
> My frame was not hidden from you when I was made in the secret place,
> when I was woven together in the depths of the earth.
> Your eyes saw my unformed body;
> all the days ordained for me were written in your book before one of them came to be.
> How precious to me are your thoughts, God! How vast is the sum of them!
> Were I to count them, they would outnumber the grains of the sand—
> when I awake, I am still with you.
>
> Psalm 139:1–18

Later in life as my children became teens and adults, I discovered the key to relieve anxiety and stress for a parent. Just insert your child's name and realize that God loves them even more than you do.

So I waited…and waited…and enjoyed, and rested…and waited…and dreamed. (There aren't a lot of options on a chicken farm.)….Actually, when I was about ten years old I called the fire department and reported a fire on our road…

Chapter 4

just to see the fire truck go by! I know now that is illegal, but I didn't know it then, and we had a party line so they couldn't trace the call!

Then I went to college in Nashville, Tennessee and met a guy on July 9 and married him on September 9. He took me away from the farm and the trees and the animals and the stillness and the slow life and we moved to the city... well, lots of cities. I remember moving to a house that had not even one tree in the whole yard, and I love trees. So I prayed for trees...and then we moved! The next house was across the highway from the Indiana University Field House. It was an old farmhouse sitting on a hill with a huge apple orchard in the back, an awesome grape arbor on the side, and an absolutely beautiful, huge, perfectly shaped oak tree in the front yard! I absolutely loved the house, but I had forgotten about my prayer until one day I was sitting on the front porch and I remembered, or maybe He reminded me. "Remember the tree you prayed for? Well, how do you like it?"

How often do we do that? Pray for something—then He gives it to us, abundantly above anything we could ask or think, throws in an apple orchard and a few hundred grapes—and we forget how we got them! "Thank you, Jesus, for being such an awesome God!"

Someone said to me recently, "Ruth, you are very intense (extreme in degree)." And I said, "I'm intense about most everything!" And there is hardly a day that passes that I don't thank God for trees and grass! I'm extremely intense about sunsets, sunrises, and fireplaces and oceans and rivers and even little streams with frogs and logs!

We didn't live there long, but long enough for Him to teach me that He is a God who hears and answers prayers and gives us the desires of our hearts, abundantly above anything we could ask or think (Ephesians 3:20).

The next move was to Colorado. We lived in an apartment in the middle of the "great plains" with nothing but tumbleweed—no grass, no trees—but a panoramic view of Pikes Peak.

So I began to dream of living in the country again, with animals and trees, and I even dreamed of hearing rain on the roof at night, because we never had that either! I waited…and waited…and waited. Next we moved to Columbus, Ohio—downtown!

One day, after a few other moves in Ohio, it happened! On my fortieth birthday, after taking a group from our church on a work trip to Puerto Rico, we moved there! By U.S. mail! We took a 75 percent cut in salary, sold and gave away everything we owned—except the kids and a few books. That was an experience! Beautiful island, hurricanes, lots of stories, but don't have time to tell them now.

We lived there for three years and then moved to the neighboring island only ninety miles away. I'll never forget the trip. Three aborted flights and twenty-six hours late, we arrived on the island of Hispaniola in Santo Domingo, Dominican Republic. We met the missionary at the airport who was to take us to our new home. We drove and drove and drove in a live video game! Then he began to apologize for the long trip and explained that we would live about an hour on the other side of the city—kind of in the country! El Campo.

Can you believe it! After all those years of waiting and resting and delighting and obeying, here I was on a Caribbean Island—in the country! As we drove down the little dirt road that led to our house, we dodged chickens and guineas and donkeys and a herd of cattle and big fat pigs, ALL IN THE ROAD! That wasn't all that was in the road. There were people. Lots of people. Black people and children with NO clothes. I mean…NO clothes, and most everyone with no shoes. The women carried large five-gallon

Chapter 4

jugs of water on their heads, and the fruit and vegetable venders rode on big tricycles with trays attached, calling out to their customers, "Aguacates! Guineas! Huevos! Cebollas! Tomates!" And the bread man carried hundreds of rolls on his little Honda motor bike. They carried live chickens upside-down, tied together by their feet in groups of four and as many as 20–30 on each bike, swinging in the wind. I tried to imagine the sensation!

But I didn't have to imagine the sensation of my dreams coming true, the secret desires of my heart becoming reality! And I fought back the tears as we entered the driveway of our new home in Pueblo Chico de San Miguel. I wrote this in my journal on July 7, 1990, one year before we arrived in Santo Domingo:

What's my desire, my will, my hope, my dream?

What do I want to be and do?

I want to be His feet—

To go into the world and walk with those who are

oppressed

And poor

Without hope and faith

And love.

I want to be His hands,

To give and touch and hold and hug,

To be His lips

To speak and cheer or to kiss away the hurt,

To be His ears

To hear the stories told by those who suffer pain or fear.

I want to be His eyes.

To see beyond the smile or frown,

Deep down into the heart of those He brings into my life.

His instrument I desire to be.

My will?

His will to do.

He is my hope, in Him I trust to make my dreams come true.

And He did, and He is, and He will. You see, that's where I *really* got to know Him. That's where He became flesh to me. That's where I *really* learned to hear His voice and touch His face and talk with Him, and that's where I *really* learned to *see*.

Actually, that's where I learned to DANCE!

Our house was the only house with a well in the village where we lived. None of my neighbors had running water. We only had electricity for about six hours a day, but we never knew which six it was going to be. It could be four at midnight and two in the afternoon, or any other combination of times. When there was no electricity, there was no water because the pump was electric. I was the only woman in the village who had an inside kitchen. All of my neighbors cooked in big iron pots over open fires in their backyards. And they had only one meal a day, always consisting of rice and some type of meat, usually chicken, sometimes pigeons, sometimes snakes (boa constrictors). That's another story for later. I'll tell you that story, as well as the rat, tarantula, huron (ferret), piranha, and wild horse stories!

Every morning and every afternoon, if the pump was working, I would put the water hose outside my gate and turn on the very substance of life. I didn't realize before how important water is. But now I do. One morning, shortly after our arrival, I was standing in my doorway watching 30–40 people coming with five-gallon jugs, filling them, and carrying them home on their heads and as many jugs as they could carry in each hand. Some would come with wagons and buckets and they would fill them full and carry them home and return to fill them again. Until I moved into the neighborhood, they had to walk about a half mile to the river. I thought it was interesting that the missionaries before us never offered water. My husband, only once, mentioned that he was afraid the well would run out, and I sharply reminded him that it was God's water, not ours and He will keep it flowing!

He was standing there with me that morning and kind of nudged me and said, "Remember what I said about that, don't you?"

I said, "About what?"

He said, "About water."

"Oh, you mean in as much as you give a cup of cold water to the least of these my brothers, in my name, you've done it unto me?" Then I said, "WOW! LOOK AT ALL THOSE CUPS OF COLD WATER!"

"When did we see you thirsty and give you a drink? Whatever you did for one of the least of these you did for me" (Matthew 25:38, 40).

I realized then if that was the only reason I had moved to the Dominican Republic, just to give cups of cold water to people who were thirsty, then that was enough. That's what He did. He met people at the well and gave them water, and now He was letting me share His very being and do the same. I met them there, and they met Him on my porch and in my kitchen; they prayed to the God who would cause them to thirst no more. And He put within me an incredible love for those people. He stripped away all the veneer so

I could see the raw need as I had never seen before, the basic needs of water and food and clothing. He took the excess away to the point that I was so aware that I had need of nothing. I could see the pain and hurt and hunger all around me.

You live there too, in the middle of pain and hurt and hunger. The problem is you don't see it. It's all covered up with pretty clothes and nice cars and sculptured hairdos and nobody knows the truth. He said something about that too, something about TRUTH and setting us FREE. But it's so sad that we Americans don't know much about freedom anymore.

I found myself crying more and more. I visited an orphanage and saw children with no one to love and hold them. The older ones were caring for and feeding the younger ones, and I fought back the tears because I wanted to make it right for them—but I couldn't.

I took medical teams, nurses, and doctors from the U.S. into the Haitian Bateys, where the people live much worse than any of our animals. One day as I went from home to home, or stall to stall, to be truthful, with two nurses who were visiting us, several people came and said, "You must come see Lilliana. She is very sick." We entered her home, an 8 x 10 room where her family of ten lived. They slept on the floor and in hammocks strung above the pallets on the floor. She was in the only small bed. The nurses immediately put an IV into her arm, which was literally skin and bone. She was dehydrated and very sick. We took her to the Christian Medical Society clinic and they admitted her. She hadn't had food in days. The neighbors had shared their rice with this family, but they could share no more because their own children were starving. I watched as the nurse gave her a protein and vitamin drink, and she drank it as if she were starving to death. And she was.

I returned to the clinic the next day to see how she was

doing, and the doctor told me if we had not brought her in when we did, she would have died from starvation before the night was over.

I went to the children's clinic and walked through with the doctor and saw the twisted little bodies deformed because their moms had no prenatal care. I saw the ones suffering from malnutrition and starvation and my heart broke and the tears came. I felt so helpless. I felt as though "I" had to fix it all. I saw the need; therefore, it must be my responsibility to DO SOMETHING!

> Then I heard the Lord speak to me again:
> He actually walks with me and He talks with me.' [old song!]
> "Didn't I tell you before?
> Weren't you listening?
> If I be lifted up I will draw all men unto me."
> (See John 12:32).
> And that is what they need…Me.
>
> I will forgive all their iniquities,
> Heal all their diseases,
> Redeem their lives from destruction,
> Crown them with lovingkindness and tender mercies,
> Satisfy their mouths with good things
> So that their youth is renewed like the eagles.
> I will execute righteousness and judgement for all that are oppressed.
> Like a father pitieth his children so I pity them that fear me,
> For I know YOUR frame, [he's talking about me now] and remember that you are dust."
>
> Psalm 103:2–14 (author's paraphrase)

That's good. He remembered. I had forgotten! I'm DIRT! I realized that my only job was to lift Him up, and He would

For Those Who Never Danced

do the rest. I just needed to show them, not just tell them, who He is. I need to be like Jesus, or conformed to the image of Christ, that He might be revealed in me. I think that's what He had in mind in the first place.

> Just as You sent me into the world, I also have
> sent them into the world. It is not for their sake
> only that I make this request—but also for
> all those who will ever come to believe in Me
> through their word and teaching; so that they
> all may be one just as You, Father, are in Me
> and I in You, That they also may be one in Us,
> So that the world may know
> and be convinced that You have sent Me, And
> that you have loved them as you have loved
> Me.
>
> John 17:18–23

CHAPTER 5

Dark Mirror on the Wall, Who's the Sick One After All?

If we ever want to see Jesus clearly and to see Him in the faces of those around us, we must first see ourselves for who we really are. We must recognize our own blindness, deformity, and need.

Taking sick people to the clinic became a regular event in my life. When we moved to Pueblo Chico, our boys, Chris and Greg, would bring their friends to me to mend the scratches, bruises, skin rashes, fevers, and headaches. I was looked upon as the Great White Doctor, especially when they found the relief that calamine lotion could bring to a rash, and Neosporin ointment to a cut. To the people who were too poor to afford medication, even an aspirin or Tylenol could save a life. Literally, a fever could get out of control and one could die for reasons unheard of in the States.

On this particular day, Mercedes, the woman who worked with us, came to me with her sick baby and asked If I could take her to the clinic. I did, and as usual, there was a long line of people waiting to register. The line was from the front window out to the street and we were the third from the front, waiting for the clinic to open. I was holding the precious little black baby girl in my arms and taking note of all the people arriving. Because of the lack of prenatal care, improper diet, and contaminated water, there are many born with deformities that we never see in the States. There are grotesque deformed faces and twisted bodies and people without legs or arms, and our first tendency is to look away because we aren't sure how to respond.

As I was standing there that day, leaning against the railing, looking back at the crowd, I saw one of those twisted, deformed persons making his way past the people in line with his hand out, asking for money. He was sick and in a country like this there is no Medicaid, or government subsidy and no jobs for the handicap, except begging. And that is what he was doing. I watched as the people in line turned their heads and looked away as if he didn't exist, refusing to see his pain and hurt.

As I watched, tears came to my eyes, not because I saw Jesus in his face, but because I saw myself! There I was, all twisted and deformed and sick and in pain, walking down the aisle of almost any church in America with my hand out asking for help, but no one saw me. They even turned their heads and continued their conversations and laughter among themselves and refused to see the brokenness and pain. And I felt invisible and all alone.

By the time he approached the place where I was standing, the tears were streaming down my face, and I had already reached into my purse and pulled out the pesos I had. I pressed them into his hand, and Jesus said to me:

> "Give to everyone who asks you, And do to others as you would have them do to you" (Luke 6:30–31).

Because I was a beggar too, and I know how hunger feels and what being twisted and deformed is like, maybe not physically but mentally, emotionally, and spiritually.

Chapter 5

> Reproach has broken my heart and I am full of heaviness;
> And I looked for some to take pity,
> But there was none,
> And for comforters, but I found none.
>
> Psalm 69:20

It happens every Sunday at your church. It has happened to you. You've been wounded and hurt and damaged, and you needed someone. But because we all look so good and dress so well and wear our pretty little masks and build our walls so no one will ever get to know us, we come and go and never get in the clinic and never see the doctor and never get healed.

"Because you say, 'I am rich and have become wealthy and have need of nothing,'
and you do not know that you are wretched and miserable *and poor and blind and
naked*" (Revelation 3:17).

"But when that which is perfect is come that which is imperfect disappears. For now we see in a mirror dimly, but then face to face, now I know in part but then I shall know fully just as I also have been fully known" (1 Corinthians 13:10, 12).

I used to read this scripture and think it had something to do with seeing Jesus. Like He isn't here right now, and we don't fully understand everything about Him, but when He returns, we will see Him and understand everything and be "all wise and all knowing" just like He is…

I DON'T THINK SO!

What is a mirror for anyway? Isn't it for seeing ourselves? FACE TO FACE? And if it's dark in the room, we can't see our imperfections! But when the light is on, we can see clearly all the little imperfections. God is like one of those magnifying makeup mirrors with lights on both sides.

"God is *light,* and in Him is no darkness at all" (1 John 1:5).

"God is love; and every one that loves is born of God and knows God" (1 John 4:7).

"If we love one another, God dwells in us, and his love is *MADE COMPLETE* in us" (1 John 4:12).

"But we all, with open face beholding as in a glass the glory of the Lord, are changed into the same image" (2 Corinthians 3:18, KJV).

God wants people to see His image revealed through our faces.

What is that "perfect" thing that is to come? Could it be LOVE? Isn't that what the chapter is all about anyway? In another place it says "perfect LOVE casts out fear."

"There is no FEAR in LOVE. But perfect LOVE drives out fear, because fear has to do with punishment. The one who fears is not made perfect in LOVE" (1 John 4:18).

What do we fear more than knowing ourselves? Maybe letting someone else really know us, the real us. For a woman it's like getting caught without our makeup. That's what makeup is for, isn't it? To help us cover up so no one will ever know, and even when we do see ourselves, we pretend what we see isn't really true—more wrinkles, age spots, imperfections! For a guy, it's like getting caught crying. We have to be tough!

> But do what the word tells you to do, and don't be hearers only, deceiving your own selves. For if anyone is a hearer of the word, and not a doer, They are like someone

beholding their natural face in a glass: For they look at themselves, and go their way and immediately forget what kind of person they are but whoever looks into the perfect law of liberty, and continues therein, being not a forgetful hearer, but a doer of the work, this person shall be blessed in their deed.

James 1:22–25 (ESV)

In other words, DO what you have been told! Remember that you're made of dust, small particles of DIRT! But don't forget what God can do with DIRT! It's awfully easy for someone who has forgotten what they're made of to criticize and condemn and gossip about everybody else. But for a person who remembers, it's extremely hard to be critical of others. In fact, it's extremely hard to not love them. When we see and recognize our own deformities, we will have compassion for the imperfect people around us!

When we truly LOVE God and know Him for who He really is, and know ourselves for who we really are, then we can truly love each other. We'll never have compassion for broken people until we see our own brokenness.

> The sacrifices of the Lord are a broken spirit,
> A broken and contrite [penitent, suffering, sorrow on account of one's own sins] heart.
> You desire truth in the Inward parts
> And in the hidden part you will make me to know wisdom.
> Create in me a clean heart, O God:
> And renew a right spirit within me.

Psalm 51:7

One reason we don't see more of God's power in our

lives is because we are "glorying" or "proud" of the wrong things. We want to hide our weaknesses and be proud of the things we do well. We don't want anyone to know the truth about us…but the Bible says "the *truth* will set [us] *free*." It also says in 2 Corinthians 12:9:

> "My grace is sufficient [enough] for you, for My strength is made perfect in YOUR weakness. Most gladly therefore will I rather GLORY my *infirmities* That the POWER OF CHRIST MAY REST UPON ME!" (Emphasis mine.)

> "He resists the PROUD, but gives grace to the humble" (James 4:6, KJV).

GOD LOVES TO USE WEAK PEOPLE!

Definition of *Infirmities*:

> State of being infirm (not firm)
> Unsound state of body
> Weakness of mind or *resolution*

Definition of *Resolution*:

> the ability to separate into component parts, to analyze, to solve, to decide

> Boy, do I relate! Inability to decide! I hyperventilate when I go into Baskin Robins!

Definition of *Failing:*

> (natural weakness) *and malady* (moral or mental disorder—disease)

> Okay, I confess! They all apply!

Chapter 5

Definition of *Infirm*:

> Not firm, not steady, not stable, fluid,
>
> Not strong, not dense, not hard, not fixed
>
> Not solid!
>
> Therefore, I take pleasure [the gratification of the senses or of the mind, agreeable emotion, delight, joy]. In infirmities, in reproaches [blame, disgrace, to charge severely with a fault], in necessities [needs, poverty, destitution], in persecutions [to harass with unjust punishment], in distresses [anguish of body or mind, affliction, state of danger], for Christ's sake! [And I'm not taking His name in vain!] For when I am weak, then am I strong!
>
> 2 Corinthians 12:10 (KJV)

His strength is made perfect in my weakness! I just love to watch Jesus work! Then He had the nerve to say:

"CONFESS YOUR FAULTS! One to another and pray for one another that you may be HEALED!" (James 5:16, KJV, emphasis mine).

If we don't confess our faults, then no one has a reason to pray for us and we aren't healed because we're glorying in the wrong things! After reading those scriptures, I realized that I had not been responding properly to the circumstances in my life.

Now, let me tell you how delighted I am when my husband blames me for not being able to balance the checkbook and when he says it's my fault that the kids are acting that way. And you wouldn't believe the joy I have when it's *impossible* to balance the checkbook and we can't afford groceries. And the time Chris and I got into a huge, heated, family *discussion* when I stopped for gas on the way to church. He grabbed the change in the car and ran into

37

the station to buy gum. We couldn't afford bubble gum! We lived in Miami, and I kept quarters in the ashtray to pay all the toll roads. It was possible to spend $5.00 in tolls just to go across town. I cried all the way through the Wednesday evening prayer service because he said, "I can't believe we are so poor we can't afford bubble gum!" And the truth of the matter was—we were! The boys couldn't go to teen night because they needed $5.00 each for pizza! (That's destitution!)

Then there is persecution! I think that must have something to do with mothers-in-law…and I just count it all joy! Then there is distress. That was when we lived in a war zone in Puerto Rico with open, wild gunfire every day. A gang smashed out our car windows during church and attacked our house with bottles and eggs and lots of words I didn't know. Six police cars came and opened fire on them with Uzis, and the car thieves stopped their stolen car in front of our house and blew it up. And oh, yes, the hurricane. It was great. Everybody should have one! Really, I'm serious. They help to get your values all straight and your priorities in the proper perspective. And to be extremely honest, it has been a *gratification of the senses* to know just Who is in charge of the whole mess! And I give thanks in ALL things!

So that brings me to the thought that we should have a time to glory in our infirmities—as in, "Let me tell you, you just wouldn't believe what I'm going through! I need you to pray for me. I need help!"

I can't make it on my own! I can't even figure it out or decide what to do. And I need to tell someone about my problems with my husband and I scream at the kids and I'm so confused! Please, somebody pray!

How long has it been since the Power of Christ has rested upon you? How long have you been in need of healing? Just do what you've been told and GLORY in your

Chapter 5

INFIRMITIES!

Most of us are sick in one way or another, but we never tell anyone. They say, "Hello there, how are you?" So I decided to respond, "I'm not fine, and you?" And smile really big and go my way. No need to give them details, just be honest!

CHAPTER 6

Moats, Beams, and Other Optical Obstacles!

Have you ever read a scripture and you just couldn't get away from it? You turned to it every time you opened your Bible and read it again and again. Then you started thinking about it and applying it to yourself. That's what happened to me with this one.

We live oooooouuuut in the country in a forest (now, today, in Tennessee—we moved from Miami), and there is a long dirt road by my house that goes between two absolutely beautiful fields. The field of hay on the right is bordered with a forest of tall trees. There is a big red barn in the distance, and when the sun sets over that barn, it creates the most awesome landscape. You can usually see ten to fifteen deer grazing at the edge of the forest. It is breathtaking!

On the other side of the road is a huge pasture full of cattle and you can hear them talking to one another if you walk slow enough. And I do because that is where He walks with me and on this day I was telling Him about all the people who needed to be fixed! You know, lots of them. They are the ones you've tried so hard to help. You've given them books and videos and spent countless hours with them and you've had so much stress over this relationship you have. Nothing seems to work. They seem so blind. They just can't see clearly…especially see it your way.

Chapter 6

Then He brought it back to me again. The one scripture He had been showing me day in and day out. Over and over again.

> And why beholdest thou the mote [sliver/speck] that is in thy brother's eye but considerest not the beam that is in thine own eye? Or how will you say to your brother, "Let me pull out the mote that is in your eye."
>
> [Or let me fix what's wrong with you, mostly how you see things.]
>
> And behold! A beam [or log] is in your own eye. You hypocrite! First [before you ever try to cure the blindness of the world, or just the people in your world] cast out the beam out of your own eye and then you shall see clearly to cast out the mote out of your brother's eye.
>
> Matthew 7:3–5 (KJV)

WOW! Did He have to be so BLUNT? And He seems to think MY problem is a bit bigger than theirs! And then I started to pray.

> "Oh Lord, what is my beam?
> What is it that keeps me from seeing clearly?
> Is it pride? Is it greed? Is it selfishness?
> Prejudice? Unresolved anger? Fear?
>
> Oh Lord! TAKE OUT MY BEAM!
> Fix ME, Lord!
> And help me to see others clearly.
> Mostly, help me to see those who are the closest to me, clearly,
> My husband and my children.

41

They're the ones I try so hard to fix,
What's my beam, Lord?"

    And I pray this all the time now. It's a terrible thing to have blurred vision and since it's been blurred for so long, it doesn't bother you! Or have such a BIG problem and "consider it not." I have a plank! They just have specks!

> The Lord will perfect [finish, complete,
> accomplish, make perfect]
> That which concerns me.
> That which belongs to and affects the interest
> of or makes me anxious.
> He will FIX, [complete]
> That which relates to me
> Or causes care and anxiety in me.
>
> Psalm 138:8

"FIX ME LORD!"

CHAPTER 7

This Earth Is Not My Home, Or Vapors and Other Aliens

I haven't yet explained the reasons for my confused state. Well, maybe that is unexplainable, but I mean state, like Tennessee, Georgia, Indiana, Colorado, Ohio, Puerto Rico, Guatemala, Dominican Republic, Florida, Arkansas, and so forth, and it's like I'm in a different place in each chapter. I just found an old newsletter I wrote on September 21, 1994. Hopefully, it will help you understand.

Dear Friends and Family,

I'm not really sure, but I think we visited all of you this summer. If we missed you, it was only because you weren't home or you lived west of the Missouri River. We somehow managed to visit every state east of it, all the way to Bridgeton, New Jersey and from Miami to Chicago. Thanks to all of you who have been so kind to give us a place to sleep or opened your homes and hearts to us as we traveled to over ninety churches these past four months of deputation. (I didn't know the meaning of the word before.)

We left the Dominican Republic on the twenty-ninth of April for what we thought was to be a four-month furlough (our first in seven years) and planned to return on the twenty-ninth of August. We did return on the twenty-ninth of August, but for only two weeks to pack all our "earthly goods" and to clean out all the dust and cobwebs that had accumulated over that four-month period.

The saddest thing we did was to tell Chris and Greg's little friends that they weren't coming back. School started in Tennessee on the sixteenth of August, making it impossible for them to return home to pack their things or say goodbye to anyone.

There were a lot of tears because the boys had become great friends with all the neighborhood "jungle gang." So feeling as bad as I did about it, I gave all of Chris and Greg's clothes and toys and Michael Jordan posters that lined their walls to their friends, who will never have much of anything given to them for the rest of their lives. Chris and Greg gave instructions as to who were to become the "proud owners" of their two big bikes and two little homemade bikes. I might describe it like this: it was like somebody died, but you didn't get to see the body or go to the funeral. They just VANISHED, like a VAPOR!

To try to soften the blow on the other end of it, we put little Iago, the puppy that Chris loved so much, in a box and brought him home with us. He was the only Dominican we could get out of the country. I wish we could have put all of their little friends in boxes and taken them out, or at least have a guarantee from someone that they will love them for us. Well, come to think of it, I guess we do (have a guarantee). He promised!

Chapter 7

While we attended the Missionary Workshop in Kansas City in July, we agreed to change jobs and become Caribbean region missionaries, which will mean that we will be working with church growth and Work and Witness in ALL of the islands in the Caribbean, including Belize, Surinam, French Guiana, and Guyana. This meant that we would either have to take flying lessons and buy our own private jet, or live near the Miami International Airport. I chose the lessons and the jet, but Ken chose Miami. We will be moving there next May. (The Lord willing.)

Now, since this job is a brand-new-just-created-never-before-filled-position, and since we have been on the mission field seven years without a furlough and this one was for only four months, we asked if they could extend our furlough time to one year. So they did. Little did we know what that involved! Being that we arrived in the US of A with only TWO suitcases each, one full of Caribbean clothes and the other one filled with Dominican coffee, we discovered that we didn't come prepared to stay a whole year! I had even left my perfume on the dresser and my toothpaste in the bathroom—in the Dominican Republic! We decided to settle for the school year in Nashville, Tennessee since, at one time (twenty-two years ago) it was home. It is where our first two sons were born and our oldest son, Mike, still lives—or lives there again, I should say.

We hoped, after talking with several people, that we would be able to live in the missionary home provided by one of the churches. We thought that would be great since it was furnished and we forgot to bring our beds. But in the usual way in which God works, "our thoughts are not His thoughts, neither are our ways His ways." The house didn't work out, so we toured the city of Nashville and surrounding counties with a realtor, looking for the "impossible dream:" a fully furnished house including dishes, linens, and utilities for under $500 a month. We did discover that it does not exist! But again we realized that HE does! Isn't it funny the way He lets us sweat and get frustrated and waste time looking for our own way. Then finally, in desperation, we realize HIS way was so obvious, so clear, but again—

OUR THOUGHTS

WERE NOT HIS THOUGHTS

AND OUR WAYS

WERE NOT HIS WAYS.

The Taylors, Aaron and Jean, had opened their spacious country home to us to use as a home base for our furlough time and had told us that God wanted them to share this home with missionaries. Since we had traveled most of the summer and had only stopped off for a few days now and then, we really didn't want to impose on them for a long period of time. You see, six years ago they had given us five acres of land on their farm to build a retirement home someday, because missionaries don't usually have a REAL HOME to GO HOME to when they get through living in those foreign countries. And we found out that missionaries

Chapter 7

don't usually have a home to GO HOME to for furlough either! So God was "forcing" us, by closing all those doors that we were trying to open to build our own furlough/retirement home in Tennessee.

Isn't God neat! He even sent Work and Witness teams to Puerto Rico and the Dominican Republic to teach us how to dig footers, pour concrete, lay blocks, and so forth, so that we could do as much as possible, as cheaply as possible. Now we know why we had four boys—so they could dig footers and chop trees! We figure that we can build this four-bedroom home for only $500.00 since we're coming from the Dominican Republic, and that's where we learned to build. The walls will be cardboard and the roof tin—no need for a kitchen since I learned to cook my rice outside, and no need for plumbing when you live in the forest.

We are accepting any Work and Witness teams who would like to help and don't have the money to go overseas. We guarantee a "meaningful experience," since the road we chose to build our house on doesn't have electricity or city water. Just like the D.R.! If you're not accustomed to hearing a person from the hills of Tennessee talk, then for you it will also be a foreign language to learn. Lodging and food will be provided, and on your day off we will take you to Opryland. Please make arrangements to come as soon as possible!

Most of you know that our son Barry and his wife Charlotte and their son, absolutely adorable, precious, red-headed Andrew, came

47

to live with us in the Dominican Republic for the past year, after graduating from college. They stayed the four months of our furlough in the D.R. to look after things and keep the rats and snakes out of the house because there were no other missionaries there at that time. They have also decided to make Tennessee their HOME. So it looks like Ken, Aaron, Barry, Mike, Chris, Greg, and I will be going into the construction business, at least until we can get the building inspectors to give us occupancy. But then it will probably be April and school will be out in May, so then we will move to Miami and try to find a HOME to live in.

While we were in the D.R. packing up to leave, one night I read James 4:13. I was reflecting on all of this—twenty-nine moves in twenty-nine years—that means if you live in one house for four years, you have to move five times the next year to keep up the average and GOING HOME after seven years living out of the country with no furlough.

This is my paraphrase!
Go ahead, you that say
today or tomorrow we will go to Nashville
and live there a year and
and sell our old things and
make some money
and go to Walmart…to buy new,
Whereas you don't know what will happen tomorrow
the truck was supposed to come Tuesday and this is Latin America

Chapter 7

and tomorrow is Thursday and it hasn't come yet
and we need to go—we've got our tickets.
What is your life, anyway?
It is just a VAPOR that appears for a little time
and then vanishes away!
For that reason you ought to say,
If the Lord is willing,
we will live
and do this…or that!

THAT'S IT! That has always been my life. I've "appeared" for a "little time" in places like Dalton, Georgia; Nashville, Tennessee; Bloomington, Indiana; Colorado Springs, Colorado; Columbus, Westerville, Gahanna, and Ironton, Ohio; San Juan, Puerto Rico; Antigua, Guatemala; and Santo Domingo, Dominican Republic, and then just "VANISHED." Just like that!

And now I'm going to live in Dickson for just a year,

then move to Miami next June,

the Lord willing.

I've discovered myself! After all these years, I

FINALLY KNOW WHO I AM!

I AM A VAPOR!

A vapor is gas.

It's not a liquid or a solid.

I think I might have started out as a SOLID,

most Christians do you know—Solid

Christians—like a Rock.

49

Rocks don't twist or bend,
they don't fit too well in places that weren't designed
JUST FOR THEM!
There's no give and take—everything and everyone else must ADJUST!
And if there's too much pressure or stress,
they usually chip or break!
That's when I became a LIQUID, after I'd been broken a few times.
I decided it wasn't worth the hassle to be a
SOLID Christian, and I realized that Jesus
is the only SOLID ROCK; all other ground is sinking sand,
so I'd just as well stand on Him.
I found that being a liquid is much more fun!
I could flow and trickle and gush and bend and
ADJUST
and all the rough edges were on the SOLIDS
but they didn't hurt me anymore because
I could make room for them and
help fill in where their pieces were missing and
Life passes even faster as a LIQUID!

Chapter 7

LIQUIDS have an extreme susceptibility to change of a form or pattern. LIQUIDS are more FREE, more HAPPY, more RELAXED! Even though a LIQUID is not a SOLID anymore, it has that "cohesive force" that keeps holding it together so it doesn't just vanish away like a gas or VAPOR.

A VAPOR—We've all got to face it—someday.

LIFE IS LIKE THAT—A VAPOR.

>So, in this stage of my evaporation, I realize more than ever that "this world is not my HOME." I'm just passing through! How EXCITING! How FREEING!
>
>And all those "treasures" (earthly goods), are rotten and moth and rat eaten
>and stolen, if they were any good at all
>and it takes so much time to clean them and
>fix them and pack them and ship them and
>so much money to PAY THE BILL,
>that it's probably not worth it and we should just leave them and—GO—
>
>>AND LIVE
>>>for a year in some city
>>>and buy and sell
>>>and get
>>>>other treasures
>>>>that aren't so old
>>>>>and in such bad shape.
>>>>TREASURES!

51

YES! I have them, they're everywhere, and I can't put any of them in boxes.

"Where your treasure is,

there will your heart be also."

Places we've been,

people we've met,

moments and time spent…MEMORIES

So, likewise must be my HEART—

pieces of it EVERYWHERE!

So it is with VAPOR

Diffused matter, to break up and distribute

ethereal, of or relating to the upper regions,

celestial, heavenly—dissipated, to cause to spread out

or spread thin to the point of

VANISHING.

I've been spread pretty thin by now and I have a keen awareness of my temporal STATE and almost yearning for my Heavenly STATE. Ken says I'm always "up in the air over something"!

It's kind of neat to know that I not only have a HOME to go HOME to, but I'm on my way!

CHAPTER 8

Final Destination and Taking Care of the Inheritance

Here I am again, just sitting in my "living room" by the ticket counter in the Miami International Airport, passing the time of our six-hour layover between Nashville and Barbados. The faces here are so familiar (same root word as in family). I'm not sure if it's my age or mental state, but I just can't remember their names or where it was we met. Was it last week in Idaho? Or was it Puerto Rico? Santo Domingo, maybe it was Atlanta? Oh, well.

The sights are incredible: the *travelers,* dressed for comfort, traveling light (backpacks, carry-ons); the *tourists* in ridiculous garb, shorts, skintight stretchy pants, hats, and dragging their luggage limit; the *business bunch,* in suits and ties and high heels, carrying leather brief cases; the *mod squad* elite, who bought clothes just for this occasion, the linen slacks without a wrinkle and designer shirts; then the flight attendants, pilots, and security personnel, the only ones who look like secure, "been there, done that" type of people.

What a sight, such a sight that TV seems boring, and I can hardly write for fear of what I'll miss! People in a hurry, people waiting, but they all have somewhere to go, a place where they should be. They're all just passing through this place to their "final destination."

Final Destinations—interesting subject. Just where am I

going? How will I get there? What am I taking with me?

"If your final destination is Chicago, we hope your stay is enjoyable and thank you for choosing American Airlines."

But, if you've not reached your final destination, and you're not sure just where it is you're headed…

SMILE at everyone—you could revolutionize an airport.

TRAVEL LIGHT, excess baggage gets very heavy.

TAKE YOUR TIME, loosen up, enjoy your delays, it's not often we receive the gift of time.

READ A BOOK, or write one.

WATCH PEOPLE, I mean *really watch*. Look past the veneer on the outside. Look inside to the heart of the old man in the wheelchair, the single mom trying to manage two small children alone, the young military guy, the person from another country and you don't even speak the language— try! Make a friend, enjoy life; it's an awesome journey and there's no telling where it will take you.

BECOME A TRAVELER, NOT A TOURIST. Explore the back roads, don't just hop on the guided tour bus. Don't stay in the finest hotels, but stay where the nationals stay, or rent a room in their homes and eat their food!

Motivational speaker and author Charlie "Tremendous" Jones once said, "You will be the same person in five years as you are today except for the people you meet and the books you read."[1]

FINAL DESTINATION—A full life, well-traveled. Don't miss the opportunities along the way! And if you're by my place, stop in sometime. We'll sit in my living room on Concourse D or C, it changes often, and watch the familiar faces and chat a while.

Chapter 8

Someone wrote me a letter a while back and asked the question, "Where in the world are the Carney's?" It had been two years since I mailed our annual newsletter, and we most likely had moved five times by then. If you will recall a few chapters back, I mentioned the verse about "those who wait upon the Lord shall inherit the earth." I do a lot of waiting on the Lord and you wouldn't believe my inheritance by now. Here's part of the last "annual" letter I sent.

Dear Friends,

For those of you who read our last "annual" newsletter of September 1994 and have not heard from us since, I talked of the "vapor life" we were living. Today is Monday, January 29, 1996, and we are still evaporating as usual. I just glanced at the refrigerator in my kitchen located in South Dade Keys Gate, Florida, to see where Ken might be today. It's kind of like an "it's 11:00 p.m., do you know where your husband is?" type thing. The "contact numbers list" reveals that he is in St. Vincent, Virgin Islands. Yesterday he was in Tobago, the day before Trinidad, two days before that, Barbados, four days before that, Belize for two weeks. Tomorrow he will be in St. Lucia, Wednesday in Dominica, and on February 5, he will arrive at the Miami International Airport to spend two weeks in Miami, which we so delicately call "home."

This is the place where he stayed for four days in January. It's the place where the boys, Chris, fifteen and Greg, thirteen, and I have found our "nest."

55

> *"Yes, the sparrow has found a house and the swallow a nest for herself where she may lay her young"* (Psalm 84:3, AMPC).

Greg and I conducted a door-to-door search, requesting that "for-sale-by-owner" people rent to us at a discount instead of letting their house stand vacant. We had exhausted the realtor route and the newspaper ads. We met so many neat people, even one family from the Dominican Republic who were trying to sell so they could go back home. They pointed out another house one block over, and while looking for it we stumbled upon a teeny-tiny "for rent" sign and a mutual farmer friend of the Johnsons who were letting us live in their house *free* while they farmed in North Carolina during the summer.

Greg and I claimed that house as ours, and we began to pray. The owner lowered the rent and the deposit, included lawn care and furniture, and let us move in! We did all of this while Ken was out of the country. It just happened to border the most beautiful lake full of fresh fish where the boys spend most of their free time, and a gorgeous screened-in porch where I "am still and know that He is God."

> He leads me beside still waters, He restores my soul.
> Behold, the fowls of the air, For they sow not, neither do they reap, nor gather into barns; Yet, your heavenly father feeds them. Are you not much better than they? Therefore, don't worry [take no thought] saying what shall we eat or drink or wear for your heavenly Father knows that you need all these things! But seek first the KINGDOM OF GOD and his righteousness and ALL these THINGS Will be added!
>
> MATTHEW 6:26, 31, 33 (KJV, emphasis mine)

Chapter 8

He always reminds me in such a wonderful way, just as I begin to doubt and question and remind Him that I'm more valuable than a bird. As I'm moaning and groaning…

> Fearfulness and trembling are come upon me,
> And horror hath overwhelmed me
> And I said, Oh that I had wings like a dove!
> For then would I fly away,
> And be at rest,
> Lo then would I wander far off
> I would hasten my escape
> From the windy storm and tempest.
>
> Psalm 55:5 (KJV)

And that is exactly what we had the first week we moved here. You've never seen PANIC unless you are in South Dade County, Florida during a hurricane warning within three years of Andrew. They're still showing news documentaries of that disaster. Actually, they have a new system of time down here, "BA and AA" (before Andrew and after Andrew). It happened on a beautiful unsuspecting day, and I only had $15.00, the banks closed at noon, we had no groceries (canned food, nonperishables, candles, matches, nothing, zippo, nada), no gasoline in the car, and the lines were already backed up for at least a forty-five-minute wait. Home Depot was swarming with people buying lumber to board up their windows, coolers, lanterns, cookstoves, and more. And I was standing in line to check out with my $5.00 worth of candles and a box of matches, anticipating my next stop for $5.00 of gas, and the next stop at the grocery store for $5.00 of tuna or peanut butter and crackers.

I was at the point of tears, actually, the point had passed and there was a need to add tissue to the tuna list, and I decided "this is crazy!"

I'd already lived through Hurricane Hugo in Puerto Rico,

57

with over a month of no water or electricity and cooking on a Sterno can. I had to take my bath in the backyard every time it rained, getting all soaped up (in my swimsuit), and then when the rain stopped, I had to rinse in gutter water! I had even lived in the Dominican Republic for four years of at least 4–6 hours a day without water or electricity (which the Lord prepared me for with Hugo). And everybody here is still rebuilding, remodeling, and demolishing the leftovers from Andrew. It's been a year since anyone in North and Central Florida had to come to terms with their "value system," so I prayed…and God sent the hurricane north. You probably watched it on CNN. And now the people up there have a deeper sense of their need for God and put more importance on relationships than things! Isn't it neat how God does things like that?

But the storms continued in the Caribbean and wiped out many of the islands—to insure job stability and security for Ken. That part of it is still hard for me. You know how they always introduce the woman as "the missionary's wife?" (I hate that.) And now it's a reality. I have to stay here while he gets to be with all those wonderful people of different cultures that I loved so much.

I can still hear Chris crying to "go home" when we had been back in the States for a year. Home to him meant rice and beans, speaking Spanish, the jungle gang in our neighborhood who went without shoes and clothes until we gave them ours. It meant hunting for tarantulas and boa constrictors and burning hurones (ferrets) in the street celebrations of the neighbors who trapped the feared chicken killers and possibly attackers of their babies. It meant no cereal, no junk food, or TV. It meant the sea and fishing and simplicity and PERSPECTIVE (a proper evaluation with proportional importance given to the component parts), which is hard to maintain in the States.

I'm trying to have a proper evaluation of why I'm here

Chapter 8

doing what I'm doing—almost like a single parent who has the dad stop in on visits—dealing with the kids, and school, and two different ball teams with three to four games a week, and working as the church secretary. This was the job I took until I was to become "independently wealthy" selling real estate, of which I have yet to take the state exam. Real estate is becoming less and less a reality as I become more and more involved with the people of the church, the new people, from our changing community. They are mostly Latin with a Catholic background.. There's the Mendez family, the Ramos family, and Maria, my best friend. Then there's the support group I have started on Thursday nights, and the Sunday school class I teach with about thirty-five people, and the counseling the pastor gives me with ladies who need to go out to lunch.

I'm a horrible secretary. I know nothing about computers, copiers, and paper folders (I'm convinced they are all demon possessed), but the pastor says, "You're really good with people." So I talk on the phone a lot and have long lunches with women who cry in their salads—and I cry too. And the pastor answers the phone and folds the bulletins! And I can see more and more, day by day, poco a poco, that God has planned every stage of my evaporation. Where in the WORLD are the Carney's? Just taking care of their inheritance!

> Don't you know?
> Haven't you heard?
> Hasn't it been declared to you from the beginning?
> Have you not understood?
> Why do you say, "My way is hidden from the Lord,
> And the justice due me escapes the notice of my God?"
> Don't you know?
> Haven't you heard?

59

The everlasting God, the Lord, the Creator of the ends of the earth
Does not become weary or tired.
His understanding is inscrutable.
He gives strength to the weary,
And to him who lacks might
He increases power.
Though young people grow weary and tired,
And vigorous young men stumble badly,
Yet those who WAIT for the Lord
Will gain new strength;
They will mount up with wings like eagles,
They will run and not get tired,
They will walk and not become weary.
And God shall wipe away all tears from their eyes!

Isaiah 40:21

My favorite Bible verse is, "O spare me that I may recover strength before I go hence and be no more!" (Psalm 39:13, KJV).

CHAPTER 9

When You Don't Pay Attention, You Get Into Trouble!

We've talked about "having eyes you see not," now it's time for "having ears you hear not."

> Hear you deaf and look you blind that you may see.
> Who is blind but my SERVANT
> Or so deaf as my messenger who I send?
> You have seen many things, but you do not observe them.
> Your ears are open, but none hears.
> So, He poured out on him the HEAT of his anger and
> The fierceness of BATTLE and it set him aflame all around.
> YET, he did not recognize it and it burned him—but
> HE PAID NO ATTENTION!
>
> Isaiah 42:18–23

Have you ever said these things? "I've been going through the fire lately!" Or "the heat's really on!" Or "I've been fighting a battle!" Or "boy, did I get burned!" It could be that you've not been doing what you were told! I think it's interesting that He said, "Who is blind but my SERVANT, and so deaf as my MESSENGER." Surely His people always listen! Don't they?

> Obey my voice and I will be your God and you will be my people and walk in all the ways that I have commanded you so that it may be well unto you. But they didn't listen
> But walked in the counsels and in the imaginations of their evil heart And they went backward and not forward.
>
> Jeremiah 7:23–24

PAY ATTENTION!

"For this reason we must pay closer attention to what we have heard, lest we drift away from it" (Hebrews 2:1).

It's just that simple, but it's not very easy! Life for most of us is "one step forward, two steps backward." We must listen better and do what we're told!

In his book, *The Road Less Traveled,* Scott Peck wrote a chapter titled, "The Work of Attention (all emphasis mine):"[2]

> Let us now examine some of the things that *love* is. Specifically, it is work or courage directed toward the nurturing of our own or another's spiritual growth. If an act is not one of work or courage, then it is not an act of love. There are no exceptions! The principal form that the work of love takes is ATTENTION. When we love another, we give him or her our attention; we attend to that person's growth. By far the most common and important way in which we can exercise our attention is by LISTENING. Listening well is an exercise of attention and, by necessity, HARD WORK.
>
> It is because they do not realize this or because

they are not willing to do the work that most people do not listen well. If I truly love another, I will obviously order my behavior in such a way as to contribute the utmost to his or her spiritual growth.

In other words, I must be more concerned with giving love than receiving love,

understanding instead of being understood, hearing instead of being heard,

seeing instead of being seen, knowing instead of being known.

"They just don't understand me, nobody listens to me, and I feel like no one see's me at all. I feel like a fixture in the house, like a table or chair, and they just use me and go their way. I feel like Alexander and his terrible, no good, very bad *day*, or maybe it's *life*—whatever—I think I'll move to Australia!" Haven't you ever felt like running away from home? I have, more than once.

What would LISTENING do for our relationships? How would it affect our prejudices? I was walking through the living room (I always walk through; I never sit down) and overheard one of those talk shows in progress. The dad was talking about his "rebellious" son and said, "He just won't listen to a thing I say!" And my thought was maybe the dad should try LISTENING for a change. He probably had no clue what was going on inside his son.

In the book *First Things First* by Stephen Covey, he wrote:[3]

> Seek first to understand then to be understood. For many of us, communication is first and foremost seeking to be understood, to communicate our ideas and opinions to others in an effective way. If we listen at all, it's usually with intent to reply. When we're convinced we're right, we don't really want other people's

opinions. We want submission. We want to clone other people in our image.

"If I want your opinion, I'll give it to you!"

But *humility* removes this kind of arrogance. We become less concerned about who is right and more concerned about what is right. We value other people. We recognize that their conscience too, is a repository of correct principles. We realize that their creative imagination is a rich source of ideas. We appreciate the fact that through their self-awareness and independent will, they may have gained insight and experience we don't have. So when they see things differently, we seek first to understand. Before we speak, we listen.

What a motto! "Before we speak, we listen." Love isn't easy. Love costs a lot. It took Christ to the Cross, and if we truly love, it will take us there too. On the way we may go through deep waters or through the fire. Real love has a lot to do with crosses and dying and giving up our own way.

> But now, says the Lord your creator and
> He who formed you. Do not fear, for I have
> redeemed you. I have called you by name! You
> are mine! When you pass through the rivers,
> They will not overflow you. When you walk
> through the fire, you will not be scorched, nor
> will the flame burn you For I am the Lord your
> God, the Holy One of Israel, Your Savior.
>
> Isaiah 43:1–3

I was reading a book one day. It wasn't a religious book; it was about science. It might have been the same one I was reading about "liquids, solids, and vapors," I can't remember. (Did I mention that I home-schooled for a while?)

But it said that in the center of the fiercest, hottest of fires there is a vacuum, and if an object is completely still in that vacuum it will not be burned. I read that article during the time I was going through the absolute worst time of my life. It was the hottest fire I had ever experienced, most likely because I hadn't been listening to what I was told. Our human tendency when we find ourselves in the heat is to DO SOMETHING! We must *FIGHT* our way through, manipulate, rearrange, try to handle it ourselves, but God said,

BE STILL
And KNOW
That I AM GOD!

And that is exactly what I did. I stopped all movement. I shut my mouth and for the first time in my life, I really began to LISTEN, not only to God, but to the people he had put into my life. And I remained in that still quiet position until GOD himself put out the fire. The only time I was scorched was when I began to move again, so God left me there until I became still (calm and tranquil) and KNEW for sure that HE IS GOD.

CHAPTER 10

REST, STRESS, or OUT OF CONTROL!

> Come unto me all ye that labor and are heavy laden and I will give you REST.
> Take my yoke upon you and learn of me; for I am MEEK AND LOWLY OF HEART, and you shall find REST Unto your soul. For MY yoke is easy and MY burden is light.
>
> Matthew 11:28–30 (emphasis mine)

> Let this mind be in you which was also in Christ Jesus who made himself no reputation and took upon Him the form of a SERVANT And HUMBLED HIMSELF!
>
> Philippians 2:5, 7, 8 (emphasis mine)

Andrew Murray wrote the following in his book *Humility*, which, by the way, would change the world if they would just read it and do it (all emphasis mine):[4]

> Let us gladly accept whatever can humble us before God and man, This alone is the path to the Glory of God. Accept HUMILIATION as a means of Grace to humble you.
> Humility is a state of mind - a spirit - a disposition. Humility is our participation in the life of Jesus, We will begin to understand that being servants of all, Is the highest

fulfillment of our destiny as people created in the image of God! Humility, the place of entire dependence on God, Is the root of every virtue, And so PRIDE Or the loss of humility IS THE ROOT OF EVERY SIN AND EVIL. All wars, and bloodshed All selfishness and suffering All ambitions and jealousies All broken hearts and embittered lives With all the daily unhappiness Are the result of PRIDE.

The definition of evil is: morally bad or wrong, harmful, injurious, anything that causes harm, pain, or disaster. Wow! *Pride* is the root of every sin and evil!

REST comes with HUMILITY, STRESS comes with PRIDE!

"There remaineth therefore a REST to the people of God. For he [she] that is entered into HIS REST, he [she] also hath ceased from his [her] own works As God did from His" (Hebrews 4:9–11, emphasis mine).

Did you SEE it? Did you HEAR what it said? It was HIS YOKE, HIS BURDEN, HIS REST. My problem, and yours, is that we get so worn out trying to rule the universe! We carry OUR yokes and OUR burdens and we don't cease from OUR works and there is NO REST.

"Well, if I don't do it, who will? No one ever sees the need like I do, and if I let someone else do it, they won't do it right!" Do you ever sit around and talk about how dumb it was the way "they" did it and why didn't they call me? I could have done it the right way! "Why did they build that house like that? I would have put the garage on the side, not the front!" Have you ever been in a traffic jam and wanted to get out and direct traffic? Have you ever told someone that they're in the wrong checkout line at Walmart? "This is the fifteen items or less line."

There are people in every church and in every sort of ministry that are doing their OWN works, their OWN programs, their OWN ministries, and I have never seen "burn out" ever before like I see it now. There are so many discouraged pastors and missionaries and people in "ministry," and more and more I feel like we have no clue what "MINISTRY" really means, but it's something we've got to do!

What would happen in your world if you gave up RULERSHIP? Try it! I know, the kids would never get dressed or be able to comb their own hair (especially the teenagers). No one would ever be on time if you didn't give them the minute-by-minute report. Your husband would never make it to the grocery store if you didn't tell him which road to take because it's faster that way. And how would he ever find a parking place if you weren't with him?

What would happen if we didn't SAVE them, and we just let them fail now and then? I would imagine they would learn the lessons we keep trying to teach them in about half the time! If I have told my son Chris to "slow down, you're driving too fast" once, I have told him a hundred times. So one day as I noticed the speedometer nearing 80 mph on the interstate, I decided not to say a word. The next day, he and his brother Greg came home after a trip to town. Chris was in a hurry to get to his room, and Greg was grinning from ear to ear. "What's so funny?" I said. He said "Ask Chris." So I did, and he handed me a folded yellow paper that the state patrolman had given him. He learns so much faster from uniformed officers!

Look how stressed out we get over things that don't matter, like the color of the car, or the carpet, or the brand, or the McDonalds or Burger King, or the new choruses they're singing at church! God has been teaching me for a lifetime; He's told me over and over again to "KEEP YOUR

BIG MOUTH SHUT!" But I've been such a slow learner—until the fire. Then I started being quiet. It was such a change that no one even noticed. They were so used to me telling them how to do it that they didn't realize I wasn't talking anymore. I realized it because I kept biting my lip, and it was painful. I became so aware of the times that I didn't say anything when normally I would have, like the time our family was together for a "white Christmas" on the sandy "white" beaches of the Dominican Republic.

The WHOLE family was there: Mike; Barry and his wife, Charlie (did I tell you I had four sons and couldn't wait until I got a daughter-in-law and my son Barry married a girl named Charlie?); Andrew, our precious grandson; and Chris and Greg. And there wasn't a lot of money, as usual. We took off to spend the week between Christmas and New Year with suitcases packed for the beach, and according to a friend who lived in the area, we had at least eight hotel options to look at. After about four, with no water or electricity available, we were very depressed, but we had passed a beautiful resort hotel that was NOT one of our options. I begged Ken to just stop and go in and talk to them. I was very confident in his ability to persuade and even more confident in my "groaning which could not be uttered" unto God, who knew our situation and had already promised to take care of us.

Would you believe, LESS THAN HALF PRICE! Dominican resident rate! The WHITE-capped waves and the SNOW-white sand made our Christmas one to remember. The hotel even had a special on all the water sports equipment. You could use any of them FREE for the first time, just to get you hooked. So we took advantage of everything—jet skis, sailboats, body boards, catamarans, and canoes.

I was extremely comfortable in my lounge chair under a thatched palm gazebo reading *Seven Habits of Highly Successful People* when I noticed as I glanced up that Ken and two of the boys were on their way out to jump on the catamaran after they pushed it far enough away from the shore. Ken was wearing a pair of very expensive sunglasses that a guy in the military had given him. I put my book down and jumped up from my chair. I ran to the edge of the beach, and just as I started to call out to Ken to give the glasses to me just in case they should go under, something inside (my new "don't have to control" nature) said, "Leave him alone. He's an adult. He should think of those things for himself and if he doesn't, he'll have to learn." So I smiled at my self-control and walked back to my chair. Just as I turned to sit down—sure enough—the boat flipped as they were trying to get it started in the right direction.

I could see the bottom of the boat, but I couldn't see anyone in the water. As I waited, all three heads popped up and not one of them was wearing expensive air force sun glasses. I laughed, and Ken spent the rest of the afternoon snorkeling. Lesson well learned for both of us. How funny! And how freeing. It was so cool. It had been a long time since I'd had so much fun!

So, shortly after, I sat quietly in the front seat of the car and bit my tongue when I started to say, "When you bump that grocery cart, it is going to ram the side of that parked car." But I didn't, and he did, and I laughed (inside, of course) and felt so free of the responsibility to CONTROL the world. The only control we ever need is SELF CONTROL! What a hard lesson to learn, and God sends so many teachers.

> Their strength is to sit still. In returning and REST shall you be saved; In quietness and in confidence shall be your strength And you would not. And though the Lord give you the bread of adversity and the water of affliction yet shall not your teachers be removed into a corner anymore but your eyes shall see your

teachers.

Isaiah 30:7, 15, 20 (KJV)

And the peace of God which passeth all understanding shall keep your hearts and minds through Christ Jesus.

Philippians 4:7

CHAPTER 11

The Virtuous Woman—"Who, ME?"

I always seemed to get depressed on Mother's Day when they read that Proverbs 31 stuff. If it's a normal Mother's Day, the kids all forget, and it is someone else who gives me a gift and calls me Mom, usually a friend of the boys to whom I regularly gave food and shelter. Scott never forgets.

I went verse by verse and picked out the ones that relate to me. We lived in the Dominican Republic at the time when I did this and that helped.

*She is like the merchant ships (real big). ("Mas Gordita" is a compliment in the Dominican Republic; it's a sign of affluence because we can afford food. In English it means "you are fatter;" it was a good thing there, then we moved back to the USA!)

*She bringeth her food from afar. (We couldn't buy so many things there so we had to import from the States.)

*She riseth while it is yet night and giveth meat to her household. (There is no time change, and it's still dark at 6:00 a.m. There was no cereal in that country, so I had to cook.)

*Her candle goeth not out by night. (No electricity, and the generator was usually broken. Candles were not luxuries. They were necessities.)

*She is not afraid of the snow for her household. (It never

snows in the Caribbean.)

That's about all that applies, and since I moved (did I mention I now live in Hot Springs, Arkansas?) most of these don't apply anymore since we have water and electricity and can buy cereal and groceries in our own town. I still resemble the merchant ship, though! We are much more affluent! Salary is much more than $700 a month!

In the preceding chapter, we discovered that *humility* is the root of every virtue. The definition of *virtue* is "general moral excellence, right actions, and thinking."

His divine power has granted to us, everything pertaining to Life and Godliness
Through the true knowledge of Him
who called us by his own glory and virtue;
for by these He has granted to us His precious and magnificent promises,
In order that by them, you [Ruth] might become Partakers of the DIVINE NATURE! [humble servant]
Now, for this very reason, giving ALL DILIGENCE [WORK] ADD [process of developing the qualities of His nature]
To your FAITH [the foundation, first thing]
VIRTUE [RIGHT ACTIONS AND THINKING,
Which will ADD KNOWLEDGE
[the sum of what is known: the body of truth, information, and principles acquired by humankind]
Which will ADD SELF CONTROL [the only control you need]
Which will ADD PATIENCE [bearing pains or trials calmly or without complaint]
Which will ADD GODLINESS [becoming more like Him]
Which will ADD BROTHERLY KINDNESS
[always, to everyone]
Which will ADD LOVE
For if these qualities are in you and increasing,
They will make you that you shall neither be useless or unfruitful

> In truly knowing Jesus Christ
> BUT he [or she] who lacks these qualities is
> BLIND AND CANNOT SEE afar off.
>
> 2 Peter 1:3–9 (Berean Standard Bible, all emphasis mine)

> Love is patient, kind, not jealous, doesn't brag isn't arrogant doesn't act unbecomingly doesn't seek its own way is not easily angered doesn't take account of a wrong suffered rejoices with truth bears all things believes, hopes, endures, all things love never gives up!
>
> 1 Corinthians 13:4–8

It was my parents who taught me these things—the Divine Nature of Christ. They had it, they lived it, they died it. They were my examples in the flesh of Jesus.

I had sat beside my mother's bed in intensive care in Georgia for thirty-two days after they removed the tumor she had within her body. She taught me that the things we think are so important don't matter at all when it's a matter of life and death. The schedule I had was abandoned and life went on without me in Indiana, and everyone did quite well. I had no desire for food. It didn't matter what I wore. Sleep was not important to me. I read scripture and books to her and sang hymns to her. I held her hand. Her cancer went into remission, and she lived almost two years without pain.

We decided to move to Colorado to attend Bible College. We had just arrived with the U-Haul and hadn't even started to unpack when the phone rang and my dad said, "If you want to see your mom before she dies, you need to come NOW." So we drove twenty-four hours straight to Dalton, Georgia and found out that she had died forty-five minutes before we arrived. I was twenty-five years old and had two small sons who loved her dearly. She never got to see our other two boys. We had Chris ten years after Barry was born. Michael was sixteen months older than Barry, and Greg was nineteen months younger than Chris. Am I confusing you? I'm confused.

My dad was a strong, healthy man. I have seen him lift a tractor that was stuck in a ditch and a calf that wouldn't be loaded onto a trailer. He was a strong, sensitive, loving, gentle man. One day he finished planting corn in a large field and had gone to bed tired. He awakened during the night and got out of bed and fell to the floor with a stroke. That was the first unhealthy day of his life. He had remarried, and due to the physical condition of my stepmother, she was unable to care for him after his stroke.

We had two teenagers and two small children, ages two and four, and had just moved (again) to Ironton, Ohio. My husband was the new pastor—that meant I was the "pastor's wife." We had hardly settled into our home until the need arose for us to bring my paralyzed dad to live with us. We remodeled the bathroom and installed handicap facilities and made the family room a hospital room. I had no clue how to care for him. I had to bathe, dress and care for him as if he were an infant.

The first day I was left alone with him after we brought him to our home, he called to me and needed to go to the bathroom. I managed to transfer him from the bed to the wheelchair, but when I tried to transfer him from the wheelchair to the handicap toilet, I dropped him on the floor. I tried and tried to lift him, but to no avail. Meanwhile, in the kitchen, I had left two small children, who had decided that I had postponed their breakfast past the limit. In trying to pour the cereal, they dropped the box. It spilled onto the floor, and they decided to pour the milk and honey over it there instead of being limited to a bowl. I ran through the kitchen on my way out the back door to ask our neighbor to please come help, and I almost killed myself as I slipped on the kitchen floor, flowing with milk and honey.

It's hard to express the feelings and emotions that occurred during those years. The feelings of frustration, inadequacy, desperation. I would go for many nights without sleep. My dad would call out to me all during the night, and when I would come, he would say, "I just wanted to know where you were." I had to find someone to watch things just so I could take a shower. I had to hire someone to come in and care for my dad so I could buy groceries or go watch our teenagers play ball. I had absolutely no time for myself. I even kept my friend's two children one day a week, so she would keep mine one day. I felt like I was learning the true meaning of insanity, and all the while, I was trying to be a good "pastor's wife" and keep it all together.

One day as I was trying to prepare dinner, my dad kept calling to me from his room. When I went to him, he would say, "Where are you? What are you doing?" I explained that I was very busy cooking, and please don't call me anymore unless you need something. I was so busy, I seemed to never get it all done. There was the endless laundry from four boys and the sheets from my dad's bed that had to be changed so often. He called out to me again, and I ignored his call. He continued to call, and finally I pulled the pan from the burner and stomped into his room. He sensed my frustration and apologized for calling me, saying, "I just need a glass of water." As I turned to get it, I realized it wasn't his voice that I heard. It was the voice of Christ Himself as He said, "And as much as you give a cup of cold water to the least of these, you have done it unto me."

From that day on, I never gave my dad another cup of water; I gave it to Jesus! It changed everything in my attitude. I fed Jesus his food. I bathed Jesus. I cared for Jesus. And for the first time, I realized why my dad had to

Chapter 11

suffer. I couldn't understand it before. He had been such a wonderful person. Why did he need to go through this? Now I knew. He had to suffer and die FOR ME! All my life he had taught me how to live. Now he was teaching me how to die! He was suffering for my benefit!

Remember the definition of patience? It's bearing pains or trials calmly or without complaint. That's what he did. That's where we get "patients" in hospitals. My dad was constantly apologizing for bothering me. He NEVER complained. He was so grateful for everything. Truly, Christ became flesh and dwelt in my home. He taught me how to deny myself and think of others. He taught me faith, virtue (how to think and act, right), knowledge (clear perception), self-control, patience, kindness, and unconditional love.

Not only was my dad there for me, but for every member of my family. My children learned so much from their grandpa. One morning I woke up astonishingly rested and realized that I had slept the whole night without going downstairs to comfort my dad or answer his calls for me. I got out of bed and went to check on him, and to my surprise, Michael, the oldest, seventeen at the time, was sound asleep, sitting in the chair beside my dad's bed. He was holding his hand as they both slept.

I gently shook him and asked, "What happened? It's time to get ready for school. Why are you here?"

He said, "Didn't you hear Grandpa calling you during the night?"

I said, "No, I didn't."

He said, "After he called and called and didn't stop, I came upstairs to see what was wrong, and all he wanted to do was hold my hand, so I sat down and held his hand, and he went to sleep." Michael had been there all night, just holding his hand.

That's why Jesus keeps calling us as well. He just wants to hold our hand. He won't stop calling until we hear Him and come to Him, and then we can rest. When Jesus touched them, they were healed. When we touch Him, we are healed. My dad became Jesus to me. He suffered patiently, without complaining, so that I might be healed. He suffered for me.

Our church had planned for over a year to take a Work and Witness trip to Haiti, but because of political corruption and other things happening in that country, they decided to go to Puerto Rico instead. I was determined to go along, but what a difficult thing to do! I had to arrange for people to keep four children and my handicapped dad. It was down to the wire, but I made it!

While on that trip, my heart was broken for the needs I saw. There were twenty-five of us in a two-bedroom, one bath house in a small village. We added an additional shower out back! I loved it! I loved the chickens walking through the house, the lizards on the walls, the birds in the trees, the ocean across the street! I never wanted to leave!

So on our way back to the airport and home to Ohio, the team stopped to have lunch with the district superintendent of all the churches in Puerto Rico. In his conversation he said, "Please help me to pray for a pastor for our English-speaking church in San Juan. We really need a pastor there and have not been able to find someone." I immediately said with extreme excitement, "WE WILL TAKE IT!" Everyone laughed. But in three months we were moving in with our two suitcases each! And we understood the reason for Haiti having problems! God used the problems in a whole country to get us to the place he wanted us to be! Those Red Sea stories are true, you know! This was just the beginning of our adventurous journeys.

We knew that it was God's will for us to move to Puerto Rico and become "special assigned" missionaries after that

Chapter 11

trip. When we explained it to my dad, he was so excited. He said, "Your mother would be so happy. She prayed for years that God would send laborers into the harvest." He was so pleased and understood what we were doing. He held our hands and prayed for us. We arranged for him to be in a long-term care facility in Georgia nearer to my brother and near his brothers, who were so excited to be with him again. They promised to visit him daily. The day that we arrived at his new residence, his brothers, nephews, and old friends were there to greet him, and it was a wonderful reunion. It had been three years since he had seen them.

We arrived in Puerto Rico on my fortieth birthday, one week after we left my dad in Georgia. It was the same week our son Barry graduated from high school, and we had a reception for him the day before they came to take all the furniture we had sold. We truly had left father and mother and brothers and sisters and house and land. We had used no excuses to avoid the call that we felt deep within. But on the day we arrived in Puerto Rico—my birthday—my dad, Sam Wheat, decided he had finished his assignment. He had successfully taught me how to live and now how to die. His work was finished.

> "And the word became flesh and dwelled among us, and we beheld his glory, the glory of the only begotten of the Father, full of grace and truth"
>
> (John 1:14).

CHAPTER 12

The Journey Home—My Story! Well, It's Really His-Story

Give thanks to the Lord, for he is good; His love endures forever.
Let the redeemed of the Lord tell their story!
those He redeemed from the hand of the foe,
those he gathered from the lands from east and west,
from North and South
Some wandered in desert wastelands,
finding no way to a city where they could settle.
They were hungry and thirsty, and their lives ebbed away.
Then they cried out to the Lord in their trouble and He delivered them from their distress.
He led them by a straight way to a city where they could settle.
Let them give thanks to the Lord for His unfailing love and His
wonderful deeds for mankind,
for He satisfies the thirsty
and fills the hungry with good things
He turned the desert into pools of water
and the parched ground into flowing springs;
there He brought the hungry to live,
and they found a city where they could settle.

Chapter 12

Psalm 107:1–9, 35

(Settle: to establish a residence or colony, a group of people who settle together in a new place.)

We were living in our "friends and family" built house in "the big woods," as our little grandson Andrew called it, in Dixon, Tennessee when the phone rang and the district superintendent from Arkansas called and said, "The members of First Church of the Nazarene in Hot Springs, Arkansas requested that you consider becoming their pastor!"

We had been in Arkansas to speak as missionaries when we were on deputation (home assignment) to raise money for the mission work. I had been the speaker for their district women's retreat the previous year, so they knew us. We had shared "our unfinished story" with them.

The response from the district superintendent when the church board asked to interview us was, "They won't come because they are missionaries."

My response was "because we are missionaries, we will be there tomorrow!"

My husband was still the Caribbean region Work and Witness coordinator and was asked recently to include SPANISH HARLEM! IN NEW YORK! ARE YOU KIDDING ME? Hey! You still have a family! Two teenage boys and two adult sons and three grandkids by now! And we need a daddy around here! And we were still living on a missionary salary and we weren't in a third world country anymore, with papaya, banana, avocados, oranges, lemons, and chickens in our backyard.

Ken had just returned from a horrible boat accident in Guyana, where a boatload of medical personnel and construction team collided with a barge in the middle of the

81

night as they left the village where they had been working. You have to go out with the tide and that is at night.

It was the same river Ken and I had to jump ship (canoe) in the middle of the night into the piranha filled river and swim to shore! Then walk (soaking wet)! No change of clothes! Until we found transportation to the nearest town, where we had missed the ferry that was to take us to CIVILIZATION! Soaking wet ALL NIGHT! This was the fact-finding trip for the Medical/Construction/Evangelism team that was planning to come later. You would think caution, warning! Dangerous water! Piranhas!

Well…they must have left out the Corentyne River fact sheet when THEY PLANNED THEIR TRIP! But God had a plan!

The group had shown *The Jesus Film* to a village that had never had electricity and had never seen a TV!

They were very primitive, still hunting with bows and arrows! Wild Hogs! No one knew about Jesus! No one had ever been there to tell them!

As I sat on the hilltop looking over the vastness of the river before we ventured out in our canoe at sundown that day, my thoughts were confusing. Was this remote part of the world poverty or paradise?

With the help of a generator, the village people saw the story of Jesus! And everyone, do you understand, EVERYONE accepted Jesus as their Savior! And their little concrete church was constructed and dedicated to God.

There were incredible miracles on the barge wreck. One nurse was pronounced dead by the ER doctor on board, "no pulse." The Guyanese pastor on board laid his body over hers and prayed! Her heart started beating! Another nurse had a broken arm, the bone was protruding through the skin. By the time she was treated, the doctor said, "I see some evidence of injury, but your arm is normal!"

It was an all-night ordeal that involved trying to find transportation to a hospital. A farmer who lived by the river (only way in and out, no roads!) had a small airplane. They managed to have him fly the most seriously injured ones to a hospital. Upon their arrival, they were met by a medical team…from the USA who were there on a mission!

> Whoever dwells in the shelter of the Most High
> will rest in the shadow of the Almighty.
> I will say of the Lord,
> "He is my refuge and my fortress
> My God, in whom I trust."
>
> Psalm 91:1–2

> Surely He will save you from the fowler's snare
> and from the deadly pestilence.
> He will cover you with His feathers,
> and under His wings you will find refuge;
> His faithfulness will be your shield and
> rampart.
> You will not fear the terror of night,
> nor the pestilence that stalks in the darkness,
> nor the plague that destroys at midday….
> If you say, "The Lord is my refuge,"
> and you make the Most High your dwelling,
> no harm will overtake you, no disaster will
> come near your tent.
> For He will command his angels concerning
> you
> to guard you in all your ways;
> they will lift you up in their hands,
> so that you will not strike your foot against a
> stone.
> You will tread on the lion and cobra;
> you will trample the great lion and the serpent.

For Those Who Never Danced

"Because He loves me," says the Lord, "I will rescue him:
I will protect him, for he acknowledges my Name.
He will call on me, and I will answer him;
I will be with him in trouble.
I will deliver him and honor him.
With long life I will satisfy him and show him my salvation."

Psalm 91:3–6, 9–16

It took several days for my husband to leave the country and arrive home. This all transpired just before the call from Arkansas. My husband told the district superintendent that we would pray about it and let him know. I said, "I have prayed about it, and we are going!" It was a direct answer to prayer and perfect timing.

This is where Psalm 107:35 comes in…pools of water and flowing springs!

"Welcome to beautiful Hot Springs, Arkansas! We are so excited that you chose our wonderful city for your convention! We have so much to offer! You must visit Garvin Woodland Gardens and Magic Springs Theme and Water Park, and the Mid-America Science Museum. We are surrounded by mountains, trails for hiking and biking, we have lakes and rivers for your boating, fishing and water sports enjoyment, there are shops and a huge variety of restaurants. For hundreds of years, people from all over the world have been coming to our city for healing in the hot mineral waters of the Historic Bathhouse Row in downtown Hot Springs National Park—the first national park in the United States. So don't forget to take a bath before you head back home!"

That is part of the "Welcome to Hot Springs" greeting

Chapter 12

that I gave to hundreds of conference and convention goers after I became mayor of the beautiful city. Yes, you read that right! Mayor! Now, how did a chicken farmer's daughter from Georgia, a missionary from Piranha-filled waters in Guyana, become the mayor of any city? I hope I can explain it briefly...

Our boys grew up, moved out. Barry was the only one to marry at a "normal" age. And that's another "God did a thing" story. I'll try to tell it briefly. He had a full football scholarship to college in Kansas City, Missouri. He and some other players were out together in downtown KC, and would you believe they ran into a group of "cute" girls? It was a random meeting in downtown Kansas City... they began to talk. You know how it goes with college kids. "Hi, what's your name, where are you from..." type of conversation. Barry, being kind of confused with the question, "where are you from?" said, "I guess I'm from Puerto Rico. That's where my family lives."

She responded, "Oh really? I was born in Puerto Rico, but I haven't been back in years. My grandparents were missionaries and pastored an English-speaking church in San Juan."

Barry looked surprised and asked, "What is the name of the church?"

When she replied, "Calvary, in Rio Piedras," she said he looked totally shocked!

"That's my church!" They discovered that her room was the same room that was his all summer! What a coincidence!...NOT!

Do you see it yet? Do you hear it? God is the one who orchestrates the rhythm, the flow, the beat, the timing, the music that we dance to throughout our lives. Sometimes it's instrumental; we have no words to describe it. Sometimes it's the blues, like "Nobody Knows the Troubles I've Seen." Or it may be classical, country, folk, Latin, gospel, or hard rock (you know, like between a rock and a hard place? Been there, done that!). For us, there was a lot of Salsa (not the sauce) and merengue—a Caribbean style of dance music typically in double and triple time, chiefly associated with Dominica and Haiti. A style of dancing associated with alternating long and short stiff-legged steps!

"Trust in the Lord with all your heart and lean not on your own understanding. In all your ways acknowledge Him and He will direct your path" (Proverbs 3:5–6). This is the verse my mom taught me on the chicken farm! And I realized that if we had not trusted God and obeyed His call to "GO" (to Puerto Rico) and make disciples, then when our son met a "random" girl on the street in downtown Kansas City, it would have meant nothing to him that she was born in Puerto Rico. And her grandparents pastored an English-speaking church in Rio Piedras! And her family would not have invited him in to share Christmas and holidays because he was a missionary kid away from home, and they probably would not have married and had three of the most wonderful grandchildren…for us! Key words: TRUST, OBEY. Just remember, the choices of parents affect generations of their children. Check out biblical history. The whole Bible is written about families and their relationships!

Then the other three boys moved to Hollywood to become rich and famous! And oh my, what a trip! Too much to even write about! That will have to be another book…or a movie. They seem to be into movies. One of them created and directed a reality TV show. One married a Disney star. One wrote the screenplay and directed a movie—I have to throw this in because it's the only movie I've ever been in! (Third row back, right side in the funeral scene; we are professional funeral goers!) Michael was the screenwriter and director for *The Same Kind of Different as Me*…you must see it!

Chapter 12

I blame myself; well, maybe I blame my husband too for their move to Hollywood. I need therapy! Maybe it's because we were so poor during their developing years. You know, you only had two pairs of shoes, and most of their clothes were hand-me-downs. But God pulled that off pretty well, too.

I remember once when it was about time for school to start, and they didn't have any school clothes that fit from the previous year. I said, "Let's pray about it!" We did that often! So we got down beside their bed and prayed for school clothes. He came through again! (As usual.) The boxes came from Patty, my best friend in Ohio who had two boys just a little older than our two boys. She sent really nice clothes! Chris came home from school one day and said, "Mom, everyone thinks we are rich." I said, "What? How come!" He said, "Because of the clothes we wear!" Thank you, God, and Patty!

Anyway, we were very poor! We made $700 a month, but we had a house provided, and a well, and a generator… but that was stolen, and the well didn't pump when the electricity was off. Oh well, we adapted. I think the boys determined they would never be poor again, so they had to "prove" something. That took them all on their own journey to know God. He's still working on them…and me. Barry and Charlie (Charlotte) became missionaries in Argentina, Paraguay, Ecuador, then back to the States to collect all of our adult grandchildren and three great grandchildren to live near them in Arizona!

And I bocame mayor of Hot Springs, Arkansas…after a few interesting paths. They all lead us to Him, the Path Maker, Music Director, Dance Instructor. The kids were gone! Just like that! Being a pastor's wife was a calling for sure, but my heart was still "out there." Most of the people in the churches want programs, stuff to do, meetings, potlucks, rearranging the furniture, bulletins, and their kind of music.

When I saw the ad in the paper for a Court Appointed Special Advocate for abused and neglected children (CASA), the tears came and I had to sign up![5] So I made home visits, "investigated" people and places, and went to court and made reports. When the judge couldn't find placements for the "tough" cases, I said, "Send them home with me! I'll take them! I've had four jungle kids; I can do this!" The nerve of that judge to say I wasn't trained!

So I took hours and hours of intense training to deal with "therapeutic" foster kids—the ones who would normally be in a locked down facility, but the goal was for them to learn what being a part of a "normal"(ha ha) family is like. I've been spit on, growled at, kicked, hit, hair pulled, screamed at, and I was trained so well that I didn't kill any of them. But I did burn out after a few years and took a break. I decided to "enrich myself" by auditing a few classes at the local community college to restore brain cells. I think a few of them left with the pulling of my hair!

I took Spanish just to keep up with what ten years in Latin countries had tried to accomplish. Interesting how they teach English in American schools for twelve years and many people still butcher the language. I was forty years old when I started learning Spanish! Anyway, I took algebra, because I'm horrible with numbers, and I heard that taking a foreign language and math helps to keep your brain cells active…and blueberries, I ate blueberries!

I also added local and state government. I have no clue why, probably because I knew the professor who was a former mayor of a nearby city. It was in that class that I was required to attend city board meetings. I was in shock! The city board was out of control! Do you remember Boss Hog and Hazard County? Some of you have no clue. You are too young. Remember, I started this book before cell phones and the Internet! But it was terrible! The mayor was

Chapter 12

drunk! They screamed at each other back-and-forth, and the citizens were told to sit down and shut up! It was there that I made the comment, "I'm running for mayor! I don't know anything about stormwater drain off, sanitation, or emergency management, but I can learn, and I know how to be NICE!" My campaign T-shirt said, "Hot Springs has been Ruth-less long enough! Vote for Ruth Carney!" I won two four-year terms!

The "powers that be" couldn't believe it. I was not supposed to win! I messed up their system, and believe me, they had one! The good old boys had been around since the Bonnie and Clyde, Al Capone days, and they ran the city! The mafia still exists. The racetrack and casino are still growing, and they always get anything they ask for and protection from anything that might hinder their "game." Human trafficking wasn't talked about much, but now we know that casinos are number one trafficking locations. But with the help of my friend Melissa, the county's Human Trafficking Task Force was created even before the state had one. We organized conferences and training with O.U.R. (Operation Underground Railroad) before the movie "The Sound of Freedom" was made featuring their organization. Our police, sheriffs, medical staff, schools, citizens, and civic groups have all had opportunity for training. WE CAN make a difference! Buy the T-shirt, if nothing else! Donate money or backpacks full of clothes, toiletries, and snacks for children who are rescued. God's children are not for sale!

CHAPTER 13

He Put a New Song in My Heart—A Song of Praise

Protect your children! Know the signs of a "groomer." I learned too late to save our son, Chris. He had suffered from drug and alcohol abuse and had graduated from Teen Challenge, an eighteen-month program. No one is healed in a thirty-day or three-month program! He was twenty-five years old when he sat on our sofa and cried profusely as he told me how he had been sexually molested as a young child when we lived in Florida. He kept that a secret all those years and suffered alone, afraid, and ashamed to share. A "very nice" man who attended our church, a respected restaurant owner who had a little boy (later we learned the child was not his) asked if Chris could go fishing and spend the night with his friend from church! Parents, wake up! Don't let your children out of your sight! Sleepovers only in your home…or not at all! Educate yourself on what to look for. There are training videos available online.

After Chris graduated from the program, the judge who ordered him there hired him as a probation officer…because Chris had been there, he spoke the language, knew the people, and had great compassion for the people he dealt with. There is always a reason for addiction! Several times he would come home with tears in his eyes as he told me the stories of the people with whom he had counseled that day. The front row at our church was filled with hurting young people whom he had invited to attend. Chris was the leader of our praise team and sang each Sunday with tears streaming down his face as he gave praise to the God who saved him.

Let me emphasize this one thing. If you have gone through recovery of any addiction, especially alcohol, which is the number one substance of abuse, then "your friend" is not "your friend" if they offer you an alcoholic beverage, drink in your presence or purchase it as a gift!

Chris married, had two precious little boys…then he relapsed! He was traveling home on a dangerous highway with one of his "friends" who was under the influence. His friend missed a curve, and they were both killed instantly. (Twelve people were killed on that highway in a twelve-week period.)

When I received the message in the middle of the night, I was four hours away from home at a conference. Our city attorney drove me home. His teenage sister had been killed in a car wreck by a drunk driver. I'm sure it brought painful memories back to him. We traveled in silence.

God immediately put a song in my heart! Only He can give peace in the middle of our storms! Immediately in my mind were the words, "this is the day that the Lord has made. I WILL rejoice and be glad in it." Peace and dying grace come only from God.

Let me express this one thing: when a person is grieving or in shock from tragic circumstances, they do not need your words or a story about someone else who died. They need your prayers, your hugs, your help in the kitchen or with the children, BUT NO WORDS, please! Give them space. Allow God time to draw near. It was Holly, my friend, who worked quietly in my kitchen receiving food and serving people and emptying trash and washing dishes as tears of compassion filled her eyes. Scott, a long-time friend of our son, took the children to play in the backyard to keep them from all the emotional turmoil that was in the house.

"A friend loves at all times, and a brother/sister is born for a time of adversity" (Proverbs 17:17).

Our precious grandchildren, ages eighteen months and three years were given the same peace and grace that God had given to me as they sang, "Hallelu, Hallelu, Hallelu, Hallelujah, praise ye the Lord" throughout the whole day as people streamed through our home, to grieve, cry, comfort and pray with us. That's what the Holy Spirit does. He puts a song in our hearts, a song of praise. Praise is the key to peace in all our times of confusion.

> I will extol the Lord at all times;
> His praise will always be on my lips.
> I will glory in the Lord;
> let the afflicted hear and rejoice.
>
> Psalm 34:1–4
>
> Be merciful to me, Lord, for I am in distress;
> my eyes grow weak with sorrow, my soul and body with grief.
> My life is consumed by anguish and my years by groaning
> my strength fails because of my affliction, and my bones grow weak.
> But I trust in you, Lord: I say, "You are my God. My times are in Your hands!
>
> Psalm 31:9, 10, 14, 15

Chapter 13

There is a time for everything,
a season for every activity under the heavens;
a time to be born and a time to die,
a time to weep and a time to laugh,
a time to mourn and a time to dance….

                                      Ecclesiastes 3

CHAPTER 14

A Good Name

A good name is better than fine perfume,
and the day of death better
than the day of birth.
It is better to go to a house of mourning
than to go to a house of feasting,
for death is the destiny of everyone;
the living should take this to heart.
Frustration is better than laughter,
because a sad face is good for the heart.
The heart of the wise
is in the house of mourning,
but the heart of fools is in the house of
pleasure.

Ecclesiastes 7:1–4

We wanted good names for our children—they have all been proven to fit!

Michael: who is like God. (He's the lawgiver, the director, in charge of the action.)
Barry: Spear, sharp weapon, noble. (He's the preacher/missionary.)

Gregory: Watchman, alert. (He's the one who stays up really late, and his house has cameras, he has cameras, he's

Chapter 14

always filming! Always watching!)

Christopher: Hebrew—origin Greek—carrier of Christ, messenger, agent, bearing Christ.

Chris is the one who taught us the really tough lessons. He carried Christ to us face to face! He challenged what we believed, our doctrine, our stubborn thoughts.

The "what would Jesus do?" lessons.

How does Jesus love? How does Jesus forgive?

What is tough love?

What is unconditional love?

What is forgiveness? How does faith work?

How does prayer work? What is prayer?

How do you pray?

How do you keep from losing hope?

Or losing your mind?

He's the one who took us through hell...and back, thankfully!

"Mom, I'm Buddhist, Hare Krishna,

I'm a Rock Star... more tattoos,

long hair, shaved head, man bun!

Meet my friends...read this book

enlightenment!....

Lord, HELP US!

"Now faith is confidence in what we hope for and assurance about what we do not see" (Hebrew 11:1).

"May the God of hope fill you with all joy and peace as you trust in him, so that you may overflow with hope by the power of the Holy Spirit" (Romans 15:13).

The day of death is better than the day of birth?

Hundreds of people came to the celebration of Christopher's life. He had 12,775 days on this earth.

"My times are in His hands!" (Psalms 31:15).

The service was a praise gathering—standing room only. Flowers were delivered from Egypt. People came from all over the country: famous friends from Hollywood with famous names...that I did not know, but they had bodyguards; childhood friends who were now adults with families came from other states; police, sheriffs, and judges, with whom he worked; and many people who had been on probation with drug addiction and crimes. They were brokenhearted that their friend, a former probation officer, had died. We heard testimony after testimony of how the life of Chris had impacted their lives. People were saved, lives were changed, marriages were restored. And some came back later for baptism!

> It was a good day.
>
>> A day of praise and love and hope and forgiveness,
>>
>>> and Jesus was there. His Spirit was all over the place!
>>
>> Enlightenment!
>>
>>> There is a sign on my kitchen wall that says, "Life is a journey, not a destination."
>>>
>>>> I like to think of my journey as a great adventure!
>>
>> Definition of adventure: an undertaking usually involving

Chapter 14

danger and unknown risks; an exciting or remarkable experience.

My adventures have taken me

on foot through the rain forest jungles of Ecuador,

with a witch doctor guide!

Being thrown from a boat into a piranha-filled river in Guyana.

Climbing the pyramids of Tikal with Navy Seals—

just to name a few!

Oh! That reminds me! I have to add the story of Carlos, the first Navy Seal that God sent to my journey! I'll try to make it short—probably impossible, but Carlos has to have a place in my story! Oops…God's story.

Before we became missionaries, my husband was a pastor. He started out as an evangelism pastor at our first church in Tennessee and then Indiana, then he was the senior pastor in Columbus and Ironton, Ohio. The key word is EVANGELISM!

The door-to-door-kind and "the man on the street" kind and for me, "I just can't do it like that kind!" I felt like a failure. How can I ever get anyone into heaven? I don't like knocking on random doors, presenting "the plan"…not my personality! Now, I can talk to anyone on an airplane or elevator, invite them home with me, give them transportation to their destination, share addresses, hugs, and phone numbers! But those "how-to" seminars, workshops, training to reach the man/woman on the street…snatch them from the fires of hell! Make them admit they are thieves, adulterers, murderers! I'll never measure up!

When we moved to the Dominican Republic, we skipped the language school part because there was an urgent need for us to move from Puerto Rico, where they speak Spanglish and I took Berlitz (an immersive language course on cassettes) and, Lord, have mercy, I'm from Georgia!

At least I understood Spanglish!

I couldn't talk with anyone in the Dominican Republic! So the plan was for me to attend a Spanish academy in Guatemala since the kids were attending an English-speaking school and had already become fluent in Spanish by playing ball in the neighborhood, which is the most efficient and fastest way to learn a language. But a few words were unacceptable, and how was I to know unless the neighbor down the street told me?

"The pastor's kids are using words that should not be uttered!"

My husband had so much work to get started with work teams arriving from the States, so I was chosen to lead the way, alone, to a Spanish academy in Guatemala. How do I make this long story short? Another book?

So it was total immersion, no English allowed in the home! I arrived and was taken to live with a little Guatemalan family. Mom, two children, grandma, and house girl/cook all slept in the same tiny room with wall-to-wall beds. I was given the storage room/closet with a twin bed, small desk, chair, and a nail on the wall for my clothes. The kitchen, dining, and bath were outside (the bath was enclosed), with the chickens and clotheslines and pila (kitchen sink, laundry). My house host told me later, after certain events occurred, that I was assigned to another home, but at the last minute on the day of my arrival, she switched me to her home. She didn't know why, but felt God spoke to her to have me in her home. Interesting....

Then the only real bedroom with a window and closet and full-size bed was where Carlos stayed. He got there

Chapter 14

first! His name is Charles, but we all went Latin, so his new name was Carlos! A good name for him. My name is Rut—without the H and roll the R! Not so sure it is a good name to choose for a Spanish girl!

I asked Carlos, "What kind of work do you do?" He said "I work in securities." LOL! I thought he meant the money kind, investments! Now I'm pretty sure he meant national! But every morning he would run like nobody else in Antigua. And he had a really interesting watch. When he was with different (other) students, he cursed like a sailor! We had several discussions on the issue, and he was thinking about running for president, so I convinced him he would have a better chance if he had a broader vocabulary!

He finally told me what his real job was, but I was not allowed to tell anyone else. (No wonder he cursed like a sailor! He was one) Only the school administrator knew. I could never take any photos that included him with our Guatemalan family.

Carlos and I shared the family, the school, shopping, and on Sunday when the host families didn't cook, we went to dinner together with other students. I felt safe as we walked the narrow streets where people were continually cautioned about robbers. God had provided my personal bodyguard! Since there was no living room in the house, we did our homework on a bench in front of the nearby Catholic Church, usually until it was too dark to read. One day we were both reading our lesson and paying no attention to our surroundings, when by impulse, I looked up from my book. We were totally surrounded by a street gang of about ten Guatemalans! I jumped up and screamed, "Run, Carlos, Run!" As I took off at the speed of lightning screaming, "POLICIA!" Carlos didn't run! He just stood up, twice as tall as any of them, in his Bruce Lee stance, and suddenly they dispersed in ten different directions!

The same exact scenario occurred when Ken and I

were finally studying together for a month as friends of ours kept our boys in school in the Dominican Republic. It was our anniversary. We had gone to dinner, and for that occasion ONLY, I wore my wedding band, which was against the strong suggestion that women should not wear any expensive jewelry on the streets. Thieves would rip necklaces and earrings right off of your body and steal your rings and watches.

As we walked on a secluded street that night after dinner, suddenly before us were two men with knives pulled and pointed at us! I immediately ran as fast as I could screaming, "POLICIA!" (That was back in the day when I could run; it was our twenty-fifth anniversary, and we just had our fifty-sixth!) I left my husband standing there all alone, and he wasn't at all like Bruce Lee! God sent a biker by, and Ken screamed at him, "Help me! They are trying to rob me!" The biker got off his bike, and the two robbers turned and ran away as I was still screaming "POLICIA" in the distance! I think it helps to have a "runner!" We shared the episode with a "special" classmate the next day, and he was angry! He said, "I've been waiting and hoping that would happen to me, but it never does!"

Carlos didn't go to church with us, but I kept inviting him. He always asked the "well, if there is a God, then why" questions. Finally, after weeks of discussion and conversation, I came in from my class early one day and discovered that he had my Bible in his room!

I caught him reading my Bible!

I said, "Oh, you won't be able to understand it because it was written to people who believe."

"The person without the Spirit does not accept the things that come from the Spirit of God but considers them foolishness, and cannot understand them because they are discerned only through the Spirit" (1 Corinthians 2:14).

Chapter 14

I felt a bit uneasy because reading my Bible was kind of like reading my diary! I have so much stuff in there!

Then one night he knocked on my closet/storage room door and said, "Okay, I've been walking for hours, and I told God, 'If you are real, then I'm asking you to come into my life.'" He looked at me and said, "Am I a Christian now?" YES!

He went to church with us on Sunday, and I think it might have been just a little too much for him. It was very charismatic. I mean Guatemalan Charismatic! But God truly transformed his life! A week after he left the school, I was called to the office for a phone call. I answered, and he excitedly said, "I just want you to know this God stuff really works! As I was coming into my new assignment in the jungle of this country (and if I tell you where, I will have to kill you), I passed a church on the road and I thought, I'm going to get some way to go to that church on Sunday! I did, and when I walked into the church, sitting there was my commanding officer!"

God goes before us, always!

"In all your ways acknowledge Him

and He will direct your path." It's a promise!

Shortly after he left the language school, I noticed two more really fast runners in the street, not joggers, wearing really interesting watches. When they came to class, I said to one,

"You're not a bird, you're not a plane,

but you're faster than a speeding bullet,

more powerful than a locomotive,

able to leap tall buildings in a single bound!"

He responded, "You must be Ruth.

Charles said we could talk with you."

LOL! (Laugh Out Loud! That didn't exist back before Facebook, when I wrote this!)

Carlos set them up!

And God blessed every conversation!

I didn't even have to start them!

All ten of the "special students" who passed through the school, one or two at a time, had real issues with God, Christianity, death and dying, and their REAL job. I learned a lot about the psychology of a person who doesn't "ring the bell" and quit. Most of them came from pretty dysfunctional families with father issues and mother issues! One was disciplined as a child with a cattle prod! I think the main issue with Carlos was that his mother couldn't cook, and he loved the MREs (military rations)!

There was a knock on my door one evening and standing there was one of my new friends. He said, "I'm leaving tomorrow, and I just want you to know I really wish I could have what you have." And I told him, "You can have it; it's a free gift. Jesus loves you so much, enough to die for you."

So God really proved to me that I don't have to go knocking on doors to present "the plan." I just have to be available, obedient, and willing to share His love and His story when He sends people into my life, and sometimes, they knock on MY door. You never know who it might be. It could be a Mighty Warrior...like Carlos.

"Always be prepared to give an answer to everyone who asks you to give the reason for the hope that you have. But do this with gentleness and respect" (1 Peter 3:15).

Chapter 14

"Do not worry about how you will defend yourselves or what you will say, for the Holy Spirit will teach you at the time what you should say" (Luke 12:11–12).

A little follow up to the Guatemalan story...about a year later as we were settled in the Dominican Republic hosting back-to-back groups of twenty-five or more Work and Witness teams, the phone rang, and a familiar voice said, "Hello Rut." He didn't have to say, "This is Carlos." I could never forget that voice. He said, "I'm here in the Dominican Republic!" I said, "What are you doing here?" He said, "If I tell you, I'll have to kill you!"

I invited the whole Navy SEAL team to have dinner with the Work and Witness team that evening. No one could know who they were, so he instructed us to say they were with the State Department. The amazing thing that happened that evening was that immediately after the meal, the group had devotions and worship and the SPECIAL guests were kind of "trapped" to experience the presence of God in that place.

When they returned to their lodging, one of the guys came to Carlos and said with emotion, "When I was a teen, I went on a work trip with a church, and tonight brought back so many memories of when I used to go to church as a child." Another guy told him, "I can't do that again. It's too emotional for me." After all these years, Carlos is an awesome Christian husband and father and a very "Special Force" for God.

"You did not choose me, but I chose you and appointed you so that you might go and bear fruit—fruit that will last and so that whatever you ask IN MY NAME the Father will give you. This is my command: Love each other" (John 15:16, emphasis mine).

"Salvation is found in no one else, for there is NO OTHER NAME under heaven given to mankind by which we must be saved" (Acts 4:12, emphasis mine).

The song "I Speak Jesus" is so powerful. That is exactly what God is calling each of us to do as His children, His warriors. We must speak the name of Jesus in every area of our lives. His name is powerful to change people and insurmountable circumstances.

> Finally, be strong in the Lord and in his mighty power. Put on the full armor of God, so that you can take your stand against the devil's schemes. For our struggle is not against flesh and blood, but against the rulers, against the authorities, against the powers of this dark world and against the spiritual forces of evil in the heavenly realms. Therefor put on the full armor of God so that when the day of evil comes, you may be able to stand your ground, and after you have done everything, to stand!
>
> Ephesians 6:10–20

> Therefore God exalted him to the highest place and gave him the name that is above every name, that at the name of Jesus every knee should bow in heaven and on earth and under the earth and every tongue acknowledge that Jesus Christ is Lord to the glory of God the Father. Speak Jesus!
>
> Philippians 2:9-11

I have come to the conclusion that there are only three lessons we must learn in life:

Unconditional Love (God's 1 Corinthians 13 love)

Forgiveness (the Jesus dying on the Cross kind)

Chapter 14

and Praise (In ALL things give thanks!)

Just those three. If we can learn those three, we will be equipped for anything or anyone that messes with our life and our faith.

> The Lord makes firm the steps of the one who delights in him;
> though he may stumble, he will not fall,
> for the Lord upholds him with his hand.
> I was young and now I am old,
> yet I have never seen the righteous forsaken
> or their children begging bread.
> They are always generous and lend freely;
> their children will be a blessing.
>
> Psalm 37:23–28

The most adventurous journey I have ever taken has been parenthood, with the birth of four sons and the death of one. Those sons rewarded us with four beautiful daughters-in-love, and so far, nine awesome grandchildren and three precious great grandchildren. (I never call them "grands" because every time I hear someone say "my grands" I visualize canned biscuits!) Okay then, this is my chance...I'll just get it off my chest! I can't stand the term "kiddos!" They are children! And I'm a grandmother and my husband is a grandfather.. Those are all biblical terms! There, I said it! Sorry if I offended anyone. Please forgive me? It's an identity issue! A biblical name is rather to be chosen!

"Great peace have those who love thy law; and NOTHING shall offend them" (Psalm 119:165, emphasis mine). NOT EVEN ME. As my husband would say, (or wanted to say many times during his pastoral counseling) JUST GET OVER IT! (Counseling was not his favorite thing to do.)

"I have fought the good fight, [Mostly over my opinions! And letting them be known]

I have finished the race, [I'm barely walking now, at a slow pace. I have lots of milage.] I have kept the faith" (2 Timothy 4:7).

"However, I consider my life worth nothing to me; my only aim is to finish the race and complete the task the Lord Jesus has given me—the task of testifying to the good news of God's grace" (Acts 20:24).

About the same time that I started writing my thoughts on paper (May 2000), the song was released by artist Lee Ann Womack, "I Hope you Dance." I couldn't believe it! It was everything I wanted to say condensed in a song. This is my hope for my children and my children's children, for my friends, and for you.

I HOPE YOU DANCE

"I hope you never lose your sense of wonder,
You get your fill to eat but always keep that hunger,
May you never take one single breath for granted,
God forbid love ever leave you empty handed,
I hope you still feel small when you stand beside the ocean,
Whenever one door closes I hope one more opens,
Promise me that you'll give faith a fighting chance,
And when you get the choice to sit it out or dance.
Dance!
I hope you dance..... I hope you dance..
I hope you never fear those mountains in the distance,
Never settle for the path of least resistance,

Chapter 14

Livin' might mean takin' chances,
but they're worth takin',
Lovin' might be a mistake, but it's worth makin'
Don't let some Hell bent heart leave you bitter,
When you come close to selling out reconsider,
Give the heavens above more than just a passing glance.
And when you get the choice to sit it out or dance.
Dance!
I hope you dance.....I hope you dance...I hope you dance...I hope you dance.
Time is a wheel in constant motion
Always rolling us along,
Tell me who wants to look back on their years
And wonder where those years have gone.)

Dance.... I hope you dance.
I hope you dance..... I hope you dance

Songwriters: Mark D. Sanders/Tia Sillers

THE FINAL CHAPTER OR ADDENDUM

I thought I was finished, but I wasn't!

Today is the third day after the celebration of the New Year, 2024 and the day after my husband's seventy-seventh birthday. I started this book in the 1900s! It's a good thing because my memory is rapidly failing! I have to write everything down now—that may turn out to be my next book! My brain is in overload. I call my grandkids by their parents' names. This is kind of neat because it's like God gave us a chance at "do over.". What a blessing to have them in our lives!

Today, my issue, concern, hurt, disappointment, not sure what to call it, is this. Ken retired on the last day of June after twenty-six years of being the pastor of "our" church in Hot Springs, Arkansas. Our youngest two sons graduated from school here, married, had children, and are a part of the church and the community. So when we decided to retire, we told the district superintendent in charge of the churches in this area that we aren't moving away. We will continue to be members of this church family because this is where our family attends, and by now that number is twenty-three immediate and extended family members. All we want to do is attend church and worship with our family. We don't want to be in charge of anything.

Ken is tired. He had the "widow maker" heart attack a few months ago. I have two knees that need to be replaced due to hard labor as a Work and Witness team coordinator and missing numerous bottom steps! We don't want to travel or move! We did that already! So tell the new pastor we don't want his job. No competition at all. We just want to go to church with our family. Agreed? Fine. He communicated that to the new pastor—fine, no problem. But then the D.S. told us we needed to "stay away" for a few months so the new pastor could get established! This plan did not come with a "how to" manual. We were told to leave for a while after the retirement reception and last sermon. No one in the church had prayed over the choice of a new pastor or prepared for his arrival as much as we did because he would be our children's and grandchildren's pastor. When he arrived in town, we waited to meet him, have a meal with him, or at least be introduced, but we waited and waited and the D.S. said "later."

We retired the last week of June, and on the first day of December the D.S. called and said he was going on vacation, and when he returned, he would like for us to meet the new pastor and his family on the twenty-first of December...because he wanted to be there when we met. I'm a Court Appointed Special Advocate (CASA) for abused children, and I'm very familiar with restraining/no contact orders and supervised visitation—but that usually involves domestic violence or drug abuse! I was afraid to go to Walmart! What if I ran into them? What would I do without supervision?

Our son and family have stopped attending church. It breaks my heart! I begged him to take the children. Every Sunday our three-year-old granddaughter asks, "We go to church today?" He refuses to go until we are allowed to return. I told him the "restraining order" doesn't apply to you, and he responded, "I am you! I've been with you all over this country and other countries as you have given your lives for God and the church, and I'm with you now! If you can't go to this church, then we can't either." We attended

For Those Who Never Danced

an African American church one Sunday and the grandkids want to go there again. We drove over an hour for one month to a church that needed a "fill-in" pastor when theirs left. Every week I attend our son Barry's church in Phoenix and David Jeremiah's church in California, and Louie Giglio's church in Atlanta (our son Michael's pastor) via YouTube.

The last service I attended, just before the new pastor arrived, the praise team sang, "Come to the table, all you sinners who have been redeemed. There's room at the table." Well, EXCEPT for retired pastors and their families who have given fifty-one years of their lives in full-time ministry. Got to go find another table!

Maybe someone reading this has experienced something like this. We had never retired before and honestly didn't think about what other retired pastors were feeling. Especially if they didn't move away. I think the corporate, secular model is being used instead of the biblical model. One size doesn't fit all. Maybe some pastors are eager to move to Florida…we lived there already. For us, family is everything and we don't want to leave them. We ministered to others for years at the expense of our own family.

Okay, I'm sorting through this! I know there is a purpose, a reason, a lesson to be learned, always. I'm tempted to be angry, but I'm not. Instead, I feel sad, hurt, grief, rejected, unappreciated. Actually, it feels like punishment. I feel like we are the only ones not invited to the party! The church celebrated Thanksgiving and Christmas with holiday activities and dinners. Posts on Facebook said, "Everybody is invited!"…except…..

So I have searched the scriptures, prayed and prayed. "Give me a right spirt, Lord! Show me Your plan, please! I've gone to church all my life, never missed a service or event. Help me understand!" Actually, I didn't know I could stay home and still be Christian! I need to ease up on people who skip church!

> May my cry come before you, Lord; give me understanding according to your word. May my supplication come before you; deliver me according to your promise. May my lips overflow with praise, for you teach me your decrees.
>
> Psalm 119:169–171

They call it protocol. All I know about "protocol" is that one size doesn't fit all. There is corporate protocol that isn't based on scriptural principles or Spirit-filled lives. There is protocol for hospitals, the military, the government, and so forth.

Come to think of it, Jesus broke protocol many times. Jesus clearly taught obedience to Roman laws and also to God's laws. The laws Jesus broke were the ones created by religious leaders, hence, religious laws. He broke protocol by healing on the Sabbath and eating out on Sunday with His disciples! He actually talked to the woman at the well who had a doubtful character and was of another ethnic race! Protocol can divide and separate, but a life of love and compassion considers the needs of people and never separates, but heals and brings people together.

There are many scriptures about the body of Christ—the church.

> Just as a body though one, has many parts, but all its many parts form one body, so it is with Christ… Now if the foot should say, "Because I am not a hand, I do not belong to the body," it would not for that reason stop being part of the body. ….And if the ear should say, "Because I am not an eye, I do not belong to the body," it would not for that reason stop being part of the body.

1 Corinthians 12:12, 15–16

But, in fact, God has placed the parts in the body, every one of them, just as He wanted them to be . The eye cannot say to the hand, "I don't need you!" And the head cannot say to the feet, "I don't need you!"… On the contrary, those parts of the body that seem to be weaker are indispensable. But God has put the body together so that there should be no divisions in the body, but that its parts would have equal concern for each other. If one part suffers, every part suffers with it; if one part is honored, every part rejoices with it. Now you are the body of Christ, and each one of you is a part of it.

1 Corinthians 12:21–22, 24–27

………EXCEPT………

So Christ himself gave the apostles, the prophets, the evangelists, the pastors and teachers, to equip his people for works of service, so that the body of Christ may be built up until we all reach unity in the faith and in the knowledge of the Son of God and become mature, attaining to the whole measure of the fullness of Christ. Then we will no longer be infants, tossed back and forth by the waves, and blown here and there by every wind of teaching…Instead, speaking the truth in love we will grow to become in every respect the mature body of him who is the head, that is Christ. From him the whole body joined and held together by every supporting ligament, grows and builds itself up in love as each part does its work.

Ephesians 4:11–15

I feel like the foot that says "because I'm not the hand, I don't belong to the body."

Maybe I should make it more clear. "Because I'm not the pastor's wife anymore, I don't belong to the body." We haven't been given "permission" yet to attend church again in our home church. It's been five months since we were told to "step away for a while." So in my searching scriptures for the "biblical" reason for this protocol, I finally found it in Luke 4:16.

Jesus went to Nazareth where He had been brought up, and on the Sabbath day He went into the synagogue, as was His custom. Long story short—the religious leaders drove Him out of the synagogue and out of town!

Jesus said, "A prophet is not without honor except in his own town, among his relatives and in his own home" (Mark 6:4).

So now I get it! Jesus was made flesh and lived among us. He had all the same emotions and feelings that we have. He felt rejection, sadness, disappointment, hurt, grief, unappreciated and punished for giving His life in ministry to people. Most often, the source of those emotional feelings and responses came from the "religious" people.

I felt so many emotions when I was the mayor. Politics is very cruel, and yes, I suffered rejection and hatred, mostly because of my moral beliefs. I survived, overcame that (but lost my sense of humor in the process).

We have to learn and relearn our lessons! "Haven't I told you a thousand times?"

How can we truly appreciate what Jesus did for us if we

aren't rejected or disappointed? This earth is NOT my home!

I AM A VAPOR!

I'm just passing through! I can't get too comfortable, and I don't have to understand why.

God keeps sending situations into our lives to keep us uncomfortable in this world!

I'm writing this now at the table in my dining room that overlooks a beautiful lake surrounded by trees. The geese are coming in for their landing on the water—but all of a sudden, a huge eagle has appeared! It is gliding over the water and in and out of the tall trees just as I began reading this scripture! I'm sure that it is not just a coincidence but a message of confirmation from my Father.

It's the Eagle Dance!

> Why do you say my way is hidden from the Lord,
> and my cause is disregarded by my God?
> Do you not know? Have you not heard?
> The Lord is the everlasting God,
> the Creator of the ends of the earth,
> He will not grow tired or weary,
> and His understanding no one can fathom.
> He gives strength to the weary
> and increases the power of the weak.
> Even the youths grow tired and weary
> and the young men stumble and fall;
> But those who hope in the Lord will renew their strength,
> THEY SOAR ON WINGS LIKE EAGLES,
> they will run and not grow weary, they will walk and not be faint!
>
> Isaiah 40:27–31 (emphasis mine)

SEE YOU SOON—AT HOME!

I hope…but just in case you have read my book and I've convinced you that there is a God in Heaven who hears you and answers your prayers and loves you dearly, enough to send His son to become flesh and dwell among us, but you have not made the decision to accept Him into your life. I want you to know that you can do that right now!

1 John 1:9 says, "If we confess our sins, he is faithful and just and will forgive us our sins and purify us from all unrighteousness."

Romans 10:9 says, "If you declare with your mouth Jesus is Lord, and believe in your heart that God raised him from the dead, you will be saved."

Believe it! Receive it! And now go share it!

Welcome to the family!

Okay, great! Just wanted to be sure that I will see you there!

About the Author

Ruth was born in Dalton, Georgia, attended Trevecca Nazarene University in Nashville, Tennessee where she met her husband Ken, who worked in the trucking industry. Soon after their marriage, Ken became the children, youth, and evangelism director for a local church. Their ministry started there and has continued throughout the United States and numerous countries. Ruth has spoken at conventions, camps, retreats, and is involved in cross-cultural ministries. Ruth was elected mayor of Hot Springs, Arkansas twice and served on many boards and community service organizations. She was elected to the Board of Trustees for Southern Nazarene University in Bethany, Oklahoma. As mayor she established the area Human Trafficking Task Force, was on the steering committee for Bridges Out of Poverty, and is now a Court Appointed Advocate (CASA) for abused children. She was the recipient of the Hot Springs People's Choice Woman of the Year award during her two terms as mayor.

Endnotes

1. Jones, Charlie. 1981. *Life Is Tremendous*. Tyndale Momentum.
2. M Scott Peck. 2003. *The Road Less Traveled: A New Psychology of Love, Traditional Values, and Spiritual Growth*. New York: Touchstone.
3. Covey, Stephen R, A Roger Merrill, and Rebecca R Merrill. 1995. *First Things First : To Live, to Love, to Learn, to Leave a Legacy*. New York: Simon & Schuster.
4. Murray, Andrew. 2001. *Humility*. Minneapolis, Minn.: Bethany House Publishers; Reprinted edition (September 1, 2001).
5. "Court Appointed Special Advocates." n.d. Arkansas Judiciary. Arkansas State CASA

Milton Keynes UK
Ingram Content Group UK Ltd.
UKHW021418291124
3267UKWH00026B/99

9 798893 331004